PRODUCED BY
MICHAEL HARLING

I0395814

# ROCK 'N' ROLL ROLL TRIVIA

GREYSTONE BOOKS
Douglas & McIntyre Publishing Group
Vancouver/Toronto/New York

*To my grandmother, Shizuno Kurita,*
*the little old lady from Kumamoto*

Greystone Books
A division of Douglas & McIntyre Ltd.
2323 Quebec Street, Suite 201
Vancouver, British Columbia
Canada V5T 4S7
www.greystonebooks.com

*National Library of Canada Cataloguing in Publication Data*
Harling, Michael, 1958–
   Rock 'n' roll trivia

   ISBN 1-55054-903-0

   1. Rock music—Miscellanea. I. Title.
II. Title: Rock and roll trivia.
ML3534.H37 2002   781.66   C2001-911465-6

Editing by Lucy Kenward
Cover and text design by Peter Cocking
Cover photograph by Randall Cosco
Typesetting by Rhonda Ganz
Printed and bound in Canada by Friesens
Printed on acid-free, ancient forest-free paper ∞

Greystone Books is committed to reducing the consumption of old-growth
forests in the books it publishes. This book is one step toward that goal. It
is printed on acid-free paper that is 100% ancient-forest-free, and it has
been processed chlorine free.

We gratefully acknowledge the financial support of the Canada Council
for the Arts, the British Columbia Ministry of Tourism, Small Business
and Culture, and the Government of Canada through the Book Publishing
Industry Development Program (BPIDP) for our publishing activities.

# Contents

• • • • • • • •

Acknowledgments  *v*

A Note About The Charts  *vi*

. . . . . . . . . . . . . . . . . . .

**1**  Roll Over Beethoven: The Beginnings of Rock 'n' Roll  *1*

Answers  *5*

*Game A:* Going To The Chapel  *12*

. . . . . . . . . . . . . . . . . . .

**2**  American Graffiti: The Early Sixties  *13*

Answers  *17*

. . . . . . . . . . . . . . . . . . .

**3**  The British Are Coming: 1964 and Beyond  *24*

Answers  *28*

*Game B:* Rock Around The World Crossword  *36*

. . . . . . . . . . . . . . . . . . .

**4**  Peace, Love, and Pop: The Late Sixties  *38*

Answers  *42*

. . . . . . . . . . . . . . . . . . . .

**5 Love 'em or Hate 'em: The Seventies** *49*

Answers *53*

*Game C:* Duets *60*

. . . . . . . . . . . . . . . . . . . .

**6 Small Screens and Drum Machines: The Eighties** *61*

Answers *65*

. . . . . . . . . . . . . . . . . . . .

**7 Words And Music By: The Songwriters** *72*

Answers *76*

. . . . . . . . . . . . . . . . . . . .

**8 Shooting Stars: The One-Hit Wonders** *83*

Answers *87*

*Game D:* Rockin' Little Numbers Crossword *94*

. . . . . . . . . . . . . . . . . . . .

**9 Girls Just Want To Have Fun: Women in Rock** *96*

Answers *100*

*Game E:* AKA—Also Known As *107*

. . . . . . . . . . . . . . . . . . . .

**10 The Show Is Over: Rock 'n' Roll Heaven** *108*

Answers *112*

. . . . . . . . . . . . . . . . . . . .

Game Solutions *119*

Selected Bibliography *121*

# Acknowledgments

· · · · · · · · · · · · · · · · ·

I WOULD LIKE TO THANK the friends and family whose contributions made this book possible. My parents, Denny and Grace, who endured the rock 'n' roll of my teens and are still storing my LPs in their basement. Dave "Gruesome" Hamilton, who pointed out to me the importance of trivia. Michael "Nash" Rushton, who helped me live out my garage-band fantasies. Gerry O'Day, music director, 650 CISL, who gave advice during the planning stages of this book. Wayne Quon, who made numerous suggestions during the writing. Fred Hume and Bob Kemmis, who diligently proofread the manuscript. Sorelle Saidman, who provided the back cover quote. And the gang at Wanderlust The Travellers' Store, who cheerfully special ordered my research material.

My gratitude to everyone at Greystone Books who shared my enthusiasm for this project; kudos to Rocking Peter Cocking and "Help Me, Rhonda" Ganz for making these pages look sharp. Finally, my deepest appreciation to editor Lucy Kenward, whose positive spirit and good-natured patience show why she's #1 with a bullet!

· · · · · · · ·

# A Note About The Charts

• • • • • • • • • •

THE HIT PARADE is pop music's scoreboard, and since 1940,
*Billboard* magazine has been keeping score. Unless noted
otherwise, all mentions of the "chart" refer to the Hot 100,
which tracks America's best-selling and most played (on radio)
singles. *Billboard* has published the Hot 100 weekly since
August 4, 1958. Chart information for the period from July 9,
1955, which music historians deem to be the beginning of the
rock era, until the introduction of the Hot 100 was drawn
from four *Billboard* surveys: Best Sellers In Stores, Most
Played By Jockeys, Most Played In Juke Boxes, and the Top
100. (Anyone interested in chart rankings should refer to Joel
Whitburn's excellent *Top Pop Singles*.) British chart positions
were taken from *New Musical Express* and *Record Retailer.*
RPM was the source of Canadian data.

# Roll Over Beethoven

## The Beginnings of Rock 'n' Roll

• • • • • • • • • •

ROCK 'N' ROLL has its roots in the South, where a hybrid of country, rhythm and blues, and Texas swing evolved in the late 1940s. Feeling threatened by the raw energy and primal beat of rock, America's middle-class establishment shunned the fledgling sound. But a handful of renegade disc jockeys championed the new music, daring to play the latest "race" records for enthusiastic teenaged audiences, late at night, after their parents had gone to bed. In 1955, as the country slept, the stars and the planets aligned with a few Comets, and rock 'n' roll burst into the mainstream.

**1.1** Who is generally credited with coining the term "rock 'n' roll"?

A. Wolfman Jack
B. Bill Haley
C. Dick Clark
D. Alan Freed

**1.2** Who founded Sun Records in 1952?

A. Tom Parker

B. Sam Phillips

C. Bill Randle

D. Leonard Chess


**1.3** Although "(We're Gonna) Rock Around The Clock" by Bill Haley And His Comets was not the first rock 'n' roll song, it is credited with launching the rock era. Which movie was it first featured in?

A. *Rebel Without a Cause*

B. *Rock Around The Clock*

C. *The Wild One*

D. *Blackboard Jungle*


**1.4** Who asked "Why Do Fools Fall In Love" in 1956?

A. Danny & The Juniors

B. The Teenagers Featuring Frankie Lymon

C. Little Anthony And The Imperials

D. The Dell-Vikings


**1.5** What was Elvis Presley's first movie?

A. *Love Me Tender*

B. *Loving You*

C. *Jailhouse Rock*

D. *King Creole*


**1.6** Which superstar act made its 1957 chart debut as Tom & Jerry, singing "Hey, Schoolgirl"?

A. The Everly Brothers

B. Jan & Dean

C. The Righteous Brothers

D. Simon & Garfunkel

**1.7** Who had his third and final Top 10 hit with "Breathless" in 1958?

A.  Carl Perkins

B.  Buddy Knox

C.  Jerry Lee Lewis

D.  Little Richard

**1.8** In 1977, NASA launched the Voyager interstellar missions. On board each of the two spaceships was a phonograph record containing a variety of sounds from Earth. Which was the only rock 'n' roll tune included on the Voyager records?

A. "(We're Gonna) Rock Around The Clock" by Bill Haley And His Comets

B. "Jailhouse Rock" by Elvis Presley

C. "Johnny B. Goode" by Chuck Berry

D. "Great Balls Of Fire" by Jerry Lee Lewis

**1.9** What was Chuck Berry's only #1 hit?

A. "Johnny B. Goode"

B. "Rock & Roll Music"

C. "Maybellene"

D. "My Ding-A-Ling"

**1.10** Who wrote the "Book Of Love"?

A.  Jerry Leiber & Mike Stoller

B.  Warren Davis, George Malone, & Charles Patrick

C.  Hank Ballard

D.  Doc Pomus & Mort Shuman

**1.11** "Rockin' Robin" was a #2 hit for Michael Jackson in 1972. Who originally had a Top 10 hit with this song in 1958?

A.  Sheb Wooley

B.  Bobby Day

C.  Thurston Harris

D.  Jewel Akens

**1.12** What do "Get A Job" by The Silhouettes, "Little Star" by The Elegants, and "Sea Of Love" by Phil Phillips With The Twilights have in common?

A. All were *Billboard* #1 hits.

B. All are classic rock songs that never cracked the Top 10.

C. All were the acts' only entry on the pop chart.

D. All were written by Jerry Leiber & Mike Stoller.

**1.13** When was *American Bandstand* first broadcast to a national television audience?

A. April 12, 1954

B. August 5, 1957

C. October 8, 1958

D. February 3, 1959

**1.14** Which statement about The Champs is false?

A. The group was named after Gene Autry's horse, Champion.

B. The Champs originally recorded "Tequila" as a B-side.

C. Jim Seals, Dash Crofts, and Glen Campbell were original members of the group.

D. The Champs won a Grammy Award for "Tequila."

**1.15** Who sang about being "A Teenager In Love" in 1959?

A. Frankie Avalon

B. Ricky Nelson

C. The Fleetwoods

D. Dion and The Belmonts

# Answers

• • • • • • • • • •

**1.1** **D. Alan Freed**

As a disc jockey at Akron, Ohio's WAKR in 1946, Freed broadcast *Request Review*, a Saturday-night dance party featuring rhythm and blues (R&B) records. When introducing songs, he would often ask his audience, "Are you ready to rock and roll?" During the next decade, use of the term, which was a euphemism for rhythm and blues, increased as Freed became a national radio star. In September 1954 he moved from WJW in Cleveland to WINS in New York, and within months "rock 'n' roll" was part of the everyday language.

**1.2** **B. Sam Phillips**

One of the first—and arguably the most important— rock 'n' roll labels, Sun Records evolved out of the Memphis Recording Service, a small studio opened in 1950 by Phillips, then also a disc jockey at WREC in Memphis. Initially he recorded R&B artists, such as B.B. King and Howlin' Wolf, and leased the master recordings to independent labels like Chess. One of these early waxings, "Rocket 88" by Jackie Brenston (and featuring Brenston's piano-playing cousin, Ike Turner), topped the R&B chart on May 12, 1951, and is considered by many music historians to be the first rock 'n' roll record. Encouraged by the success of "Rocket 88," Phillips quit his job at WREC and started Sun Records in 1952. "That's All Right," the first of five Elvis Presley singles on Sun Records, was released on July 19, 1954. After Sun sold Presley's contract to RCA for $35,000 in November 1955, Phillips launched the recording careers of rock 'n' roll pioneers such as Carl Perkins, Charlie Rich, Johnny Cash, Roy Orbison, and Jerry Lee Lewis.

**1.3** D. *Blackboard Jungle*

"(We're Gonna) Rock Around The Clock" was recorded by
Bill Haley And His Comets on April 12, 1954, at New York's
Pythian Temple, a converted Masonic building that Decca
Records used as a studio. The song was released on May 10 to
modest acclaim as the B-side of "Thirteen Women (And Only
One Man In Town)." In 1955, however, the song accompanied
the opening credits of *Blackboard Jungle*, a movie about
teenaged rebellion starring Glenn Ford and Sidney Poitier.
Based on the reaction of moviegoers—they rioted when the
song was played—"Rock Around The Clock" was re-released:
on July 9 it reached #1, where it remained for eight weeks.
In 1956 Haley starred in the movie *Rock Around The Clock*, a
fictional account of the beginnings of rock 'n' roll.

**1.4** B. The Teenagers Featuring Frankie Lymon

Lymon was only thirteen when he and the four Teenagers
recorded "Why Do Fools Fall In Love" in the spring of 1955,
and although Lymon was the youngest and the last to join the
New York City–based group, it was the youngster's superb
lead vocal that carried the tune to #6 on the pop chart on
April 14, 1956 (#1 on the R&B survey). The success of the
quintet, which soon became known as Frankie Lymon and The
Teenagers, influenced countless "kid" vocal groups, not the
least of which was the Jackson 5.

**1.5** A. *Love Me Tender*

Elvis Presley made his 1956 big-screen debut in the role of
Clint Reno, a young Southern man who falls in love with
Cathy (Debra Paget), the girlfriend of his older brother Vance
(Richard Egan), while Vance is off fighting in the Civil War.
Although the film was originally titled *The Reno Brothers*,
Paramount Pictures changed the name to capitalize on
Presley's immense popularity: in 1956 his five #1 hits,

. . . . . . . . . . . . . . . . . . . . . . . . . .

including "Love Me Tender," were in the top spot for a total of 25 weeks. In addition to the title tune, which, buoyed by two performances on the *Ed Sullivan Show*, was at the top of the chart when the movie premiered on November 16, Elvis sang three other songs—"Let Me," "We're Gonna Move (To A Better Home)," and "Poor Boy"—before his character died.

**1.6 D. Simon & Garfunkel**

Listening to rock 'n' roll radio in the mid-1950s, boyhood friends Art "Tom" Garfunkel and Paul "Jerry" Simon convinced themselves that they could make records. After countless subway trips from their homes in Queens to peddle their songs to music publishers in Manhattan, the 15 year olds invested $25 in a demo of their Everly Brothers–inspired composition, "Hey, Schoolgirl." During the recording session, producer Sid Prosen overheard the duo and offered them a contract on the spot. The song, which the boys lip-synched on *American Bandstand*, peaked at #49 on December 27, 1957. None of Tom & Jerry's several follow-up singles charted; but on January 1, 1966, "The Sounds Of Silence," Simon & Garfunkel's first single, announced the act's arrival by topping the *Billboard* Hot 100.

**1.7 C. Jerry Lee Lewis**

Peaking at #7 on March 29, 1958, "Breathless" joined "Whole Lot Of Shakin' Going On," a #3 tune, and "Great Balls Of Fire," a #2 song, as Lewis's third Top 10 hit within a year. With Elvis Presley's induction into the army on March 24, the 22-year-old Lewis was poised to become rock 'n' roll's next big star when he arrived in London on May 22 to begin a 30-show British tour. But Lewis's promising career fell apart when British reporters asked about the girl accompanying him: it was his second cousin Myra, aged 13, whom he'd married five months earlier. Dogged by the press and playing to sparse but antagonistic audiences, Lewis returned to the U.S. after only three shows. The scandal followed him home, and Lewis found himself blacklisted from Top 40 radio. Although he had some success on the country survey, he never had another Top 20 hit on the pop chart.

**1.8** **C. "Johnny B. Goode" by Chuck Berry**
The Voyager capsules were only the third and fourth spacecraft to escape the gravitational pull of the Sun. In an attempt to communicate the story of the Earth to any spacefarers who might one day encounter the ships, NASA included a 12-inch gold-plated copper phonograph disc as part of its Interstellar Outreach Program. A committee chaired by astronomer Carl Sagan assembled an aural portrait of the Earth that included natural sounds, such as those of surf and wind, greetings spoken in 55 languages, and 90 minutes of music. Among the 27 musical selections were the first movement of Beethoven's "Symphony No. 5 In C Minor," a Peruvian wedding song, and, of course, Berry's 1958 Top 10 hit. Shortly after the launch, *Saturday Night Live* reported that NASA had received a reply from outer space. The message? "Send more Chuck Berry."

**1.9** **D. "My Ding-A-Ling"**
Despite writing and recording some of rock's first—and finest—anthems, Berry failed to register a #1 hit until October 21, 1972, when "My Ding-A-Ling" topped the *Billboard* Hot 100. In stark contrast to the timeless lyrics of his earlier works, "My Ding-A-Ling," which was recorded live at the Lancaster Arts Festival in Coventry, England, is a sophomoric ditty about masturbation. Prior to this self-indulgence, Berry's highest-charting single was "Sweet Little Sixteen," a #2 hit for three weeks in 1958.

**1.10**   **B. Warren Davis, George Malone, & Charles Patrick**
On April 12, 1958, "Book Of Love" was a #5 hit for The
Monotones, a doo-wop sextet from Newark, New Jersey, that
counted Davis, Malone, and Patrick among its members. The
six vocalists lived in the same neighborhood as, and sang in a
church choir with, Cissy Houston—Whitney's mother—and
Dionne Warwick, who is Patrick's cousin. According to legend, Patrick got the idea for "Book Of Love" from a similarly
named song and a then-popular commercial jingle that had a
similar rhythm and melody, "You'll wonder where the yellow
went/When you brush your teeth with Pepsodent." The song
was recorded and released in 1957 but didn't gain popularity
until it was re-issued in 1958. Although Chapter One of The
Monotones' story was promising, Chapter Two was never
written as the group failed to chart ever again.

**1.11**   **B. Bobby Day**
"Rockin' Robin" landed in the #2 spot of the *Billboard* Hot
100 on October 13, 1958, for Day, whose birth name was
Robert Byrd. When Michael Jackson's cover of the song
peaked in the runner-up position on April 22, 1972, the
tweetin' tune became the first song of the rock era to crest
at #2 for different acts. Appropriately, both versions occupied
the second slot for two weeks each. Jackson, of course, went
on to top the chart many times over, but for Day, "Rockin'
Robin" was the pinnacle of his recording career. As a
songwriter, however, Day managed to claim the top spot
when "Over and Over," the B-side of "Rockin' Robin," went
to #1 for the Dave Clark Five on December 25, 1965.

**1.12**   **C. All were the acts' only entry on the pop chart.**
Despite the enduring nature of all three songs, they were
the sole chart appearances for the acts performing them.
Originally recorded in late 1957 as the B-side of The

Silhouettes' first single, "Get A Job" proved more popular than the ballad "I Am Lonely," reaching #1 on February 15, 1958; the song's "sha na na na" refrain was adopted in 1969 as the name of a 1950s rock 'n' roll revival band. "Little Star," The Elegants' doo-wop variation of Mozart's "Twinkle, Twinkle Little Star," topped the chart on August 25, 1958. A year later, on August 24, 1959, "Sea Of Love" pulled into the #2 berth for Phil Phillips.

**1.13**  **B. August 5, 1957**
*American Bandstand* kicked off its first national broadcast on a Monday with Jerry Lee Lewis lip-synching "Whole Lot Of Shakin' Going On." Initially the 90-minute dance party aired weekday afternoons on affiliates of the ABC-TV network, but in 1963 the show, shortened to 60 minutes, began weekly broadcasts on Saturday afternoons. *Bandstand*, as it was originally known, was first televised locally by Philadelphia's WFIL in 1952. After host Bob Horn encountered personal problems in 1956, he was replaced by Dick Clark who, for the next 33 years, introduced rising stars to the show's mostly teenaged viewers. On October 7, 1989, with David Hirsch hosting, the last instalment of *American Bandstand* aired on the USA Network.

**1.14**  **C. Jim Seals, Dash Crofts, and Glen Campbell were original members of the group.**
Although the three future stars played with The Champs, all did so after "Tequila" topped the chart on March 17, 1958. Later that summer, Seals and Crofts, who would score a trio of Top 10 hits as the soft-rock duo Seals & Crofts in the 1970s, replaced the band's original sax player and drummer, respectively; they remained with the group until 1965 when it dissolved. Campbell joined The Champs in November 1960 and departed six months later to pursue a hit-laden solo career.

"Tequila," which was recognized as the Best Rhythm & Blues Performance at the first ever Grammy Awards in 1958, was originally recorded for Challenge Records by a group of studio musicians as the B-side of "Train To Nowhere." Needing a name, the group borrowed one from the horse of Gene Autry, the owner of Challenge Records.

**1.15  D. Dion and The Belmonts**

"A Teenager In Love," a song about the tribulations of young romance written by Doc Pomus and Mort Shuman, peaked at #5 for Dion and The Belmonts on May 18, 1959. Dissatisfied with the backing vocalists supplied by the record company for his first single, Dion DiMucci teamed up with The Belmonts, a group named after an avenue in the Bronx and with which he had occasionally sung on street corners. Although their first record failed to chart, the next three, released in 1958, all reached the Top 40; their fifth single was "A Teenager In Love." After four more records, which included "Where Or When," a #3 hit on February 8, 1960, Dion parted with The Belmonts. Billed as a solo act—he was backed by The Del-Satins—Dion scored his biggest hit, the 1961 chart-topper "Runaround Sue."

# Game A

## Going To The Chapel

• • • • • • •

Match the rock 'n' roll star with the partner who has earned his/her own celebrity. *(Solutions on page 119.)*

| | | | |
|---|---|---|---|
| **1.** Steve Lawrence | | **A.** | Carrie Fisher |
| **2.** Bobby Darin | | **B.** | Valerie Bertinelli |
| **3.** Lulu | | **C.** | Christie Brinkley |
| **4.** Paul Simon | | **D.** | Veronica Bennett |
| **5.** Phil Spector | | **E.** | Rita Coolidge |
| **6.** Chrissie Hynde | | **F.** | Sean Penn |
| **7.** Billy Joel | | **G.** | Eydie Gorme |
| **8.** Kris Kristofferson | | **H.** | Barbara Bach |
| **9.** Carly Simon | | **I.** | Gregg Allman |
| **10.** Eddie Van Halen | | **J.** | Sandra Dee |
| **11.** Ringo Starr | | **K.** | James Taylor |
| **12.** Cher | | **L.** | Maurice Gibb |
| **13.** Peter Wolf | | **M.** | Jim Kerr |
| **14.** Mick Jagger | | **N.** | Jerry Hall |
| **15.** Madonna | | **O.** | Faye Dunaway |

# American Graffiti

## The Early Sixties

. . . . . . . . . . .

I N 1960, five years after it emerged, rock 'n' roll underwent
its first metamorphosis. The sound's early stars were no
longer recording: Chuck Berry was in jail, Jerry Lee Lewis
was in disgrace, Buddy Holly was in heaven, and, as the year
began, Elvis Presley was in the army (later he would focus on a
career in the movies). So rock 'n' roll moved uptown. To New
York, where the girl groups flourished. To Detroit, where the
Motown hit factory found its groove. To Philadelphia, where
*American Bandstand* made its home. And to Los Angeles, where
the surf sound came ashore.

**2.1** Which group featured Clyde McPhatter and, later, Ben E. King
as lead singer?

A. The Platters

B. The Drifters

C. The Coasters

D. The Searchers

**2.2** What rank did Elvis Presley hold when he was discharged from the U.S. Army?

A. Private

B. Corporal

C. Captain

D. Sergeant

**2.3** Which girl group was the first to have a #1 pop hit?

A. The Chiffons

B. The Crystals

C. The Marvelettes

D. The Shirelles

**2.4** Chubby Checker's first chart-topper was "The Twist." What was his second?

A. "Peppermint Twist: Part I"

B. "C'mon And Swim"

C. "Pony Time"

D. "Twistin' The Night Away"

**2.5** Who put "Who Put The Bomp (In The Bomp, Bomp, Bomp)" on the chart in 1961?

A. Jimmy Dean

B. Barry Mann

C. Larry Verne

D. Ernie K-Doe

**2.6** What was the Beach Boys' original name?

A. The Pendletones

B. The Hawthornes

C. The Honeys

D. The El Caminos

**2.7** Where was Hitsville U.S.A.?

A. New York City

B. Memphis

C. Detroit

D. Nashville

**2.8** Which 1963 hit did George Harrison "subconsciously" plagiarize when he wrote "My Sweet Lord"?

A. "One Fine Day"

B. "He's So Fine"

C. "I Feel Fine"

D. "Oh Happy Day"

**2.9** Which statement about "Louie Louie" is false?

A. It first appeared on record as a B-side.

B. For more than two years, the FBI investigated the song's allegedly obscene lyrics.

C. It is the official song of Washington state.

D. In 1963, it was a #2 hit for The Kingsmen.

**2.10** Which song was a #1 hit in the early 1960s and then a #1 hit in the 1970s for a different artist?

A. "Sealed With A Kiss"

B. "Puppy Love"

C. "Da Doo Ron Ron"

D. "Go Away Little Girl"

**2.11** Who are the Righteous Brothers?

A. Jerry Leiber & Mike Stoller

B. Phil Spector & Ronnie Spector

C. Bill Medley & Bobby Hatfield

D. Barry Mann & Kurt Weill

**2.12** Which song was a Top 10 hit in 1964 for Terry Stafford, an Elvis sound-alike?

A. "Suspicious Minds"

B. "Suspicion"

C. "Temptation"

D. "Temptation Eyes"

**2.13** In 1999, Pearl Jam's cover of "Last Kiss" was a #2 hit. Which act achieved the same ranking with the song in 1964?

A. Mark Dinning

B. J. Frank Wilson & The Cavaliers

C. Jan & Dean

D. Ray Peterson

**2.14** Which producer developed the "Wall of Sound" recording style?

A. George Martin

B. Phil Spector

C. Brian Wilson

D. George "Shadow" Morton

**2.15** Which event occurred first?

A. Roy Orbison topped the chart for the first time.

B. President Kennedy was assassinated.

C. The Beatles released their first U.S. single.

D. Little Stevie Wonder released his first #1 single.

# Answers

• • • • • • • • • •

### 2.1  B. The Drifters

After leaving The Dominoes in early 1953, Clyde McPhatter signed with Atlantic Records and assembled The Drifters as his backing vocalists. By the fall, the group hit #1 on *Billboard*'s R&B chart with "Money Honey." In 1954, though, McPhatter was drafted, and when his service was over, he pursued a solo career. On his own, McPhatter's biggest hits were "A Lover's Question," which reached #6 on the *Billboard* Hot 100 in 1959, and "Lover Please," a #7 tune in 1962. Meanwhile, The Drifters, who had continued to record, disbanded in 1958 and then re-formed the next year with an entirely different lineup. The new group, featuring Ben E. King singing lead, scored a #2 hit in 1959 with "There Goes My Baby," followed by a 1960 chart-topper, "Save The Last Dance For Me." In 1961, King, as a solo act, registered a #10 tune, "Spanish Harlem," and a #4 hit with the classic "Stand By Me," which as the title song of a movie, re-charted and reached #9 in 1986. After King left the group, The Drifters notched Top 10 hits with "Up On The Roof," #5 in 1963; "On Broadway," #9 later the same year; and "Under The Boardwalk," #4 in 1964.

### 2.2  D. Sergeant

When he was discharged from the U.S. Army on March 5, 1960, Elvis Presley was a sergeant, having earned his stripes six weeks earlier on January 20. The King was inducted into the army as a private in Memphis on March 24, 1958, then posted to Fort Hood, Texas, for basic training. From October 1, 1958, until March 2, 1960, he was stationed at the Friedburg Army Base near Bad Nauheim, Germany. On November 27, 1958, Presley was promoted to private first class and on June 1, 1959, he was elevated to specialist fourth class. Following his discharge, Elvis starred in *G.I. Blues*, a movie in which he portrayed an American soldier stationed in—you guessed it—Germany.

### 2.3 D. The Shirelles
When "Will You Love Me Tomorrow" topped the *Billboard* Hot 100 on January 30, 1961, The Shirelles became the first of the 1960s girl groups to lead the hit parade, paving the way for others, such as The Marvelettes, The Crystals, and The Chiffons, who followed. Founded in 1957 while the girls were students at Passaic (New Jersey) High School, the quartet was initially hesitant to turn professional. Nevertheless, their debut record, "I Met Him On A Sunday," reached #49 on April 19, 1958, but it would be more than two years and five singles before The Shirelles cracked the Top 40 with "Tonight's The Night," which crept to #39 on October 24, 1960. Their next release, a Gerry Goffin–Carole King tune that The Shirelles were reluctant to record, went to #1. Fifteen months later, on May 5, 1962, "Soldier Boy" marched the quartet to its second and final chart-topper.

### 2.4 C. "Pony Time"
Although Chubby Checker had other hits with "twist" themes, such as "Let's Twist Again" and "Slow Twistin'," he isn't known for either "Peppermint Twist" or "Twistin' The Night Away"; rather, they were Top 10 hits in 1962 for Joey Dee & the Starliters and Sam Cooke, respectively. Like "The Twist," which was a reworking of a 1958 B-side by its writer, Hank Ballard, "Pony Time" was also a cover tune. While the writers' versions failed, Checker's succeeded, largely because he was from Philadelphia, the home of *American Bandstand*, and he was popular with the show's host, Dick Clark. On February 27, 1961, five months after "The Twist" topped the *Billboard* Hot 100, "Pony Time" sashayed into the top spot.

. . . . . . . . . . . . . . . . . . . . . . . . . .

## 2.5 B. Barry Mann

It's difficult to call the Brooklyn-born Mann a one-hit wonder, but as a performer he is nothing more: "Who Put The Bomp (In The Bomp, Bomp, Bomp)," a novelty send-up of doo-wop music that peaked at #7 on September 25, 1961, is the only one of his four charted singles to sneak above #78. Mann achieved much greater success as a composer, co-writing some of the most popular tunes of the 1960s. Teamed with Cynthia Weil, his wife and lyricist, he penned several Top 10 songs, including "Blame It On The Bossa Nova," "(You're My) Soul And Inspiration," and "Kicks." With other writers, he contributed to hits such as "Footsteps," "On Broadway," "You've Lost That Lovin' Feelin'," and, of course, "Who Put The Bomp."

## 2.6 A. The Pendletones

The group—brothers Brian, Carl, and Dennis Wilson; their cousin Mike Love; and Brian's football teammate Al Jardine—formed in the Los Angeles suburb of Hawthorne in 1961. In his autobiography, *Wouldn't It Be Nice*, Brian says that Love named the band after Pendleton shirts, which were popular in southern California at the time. The quintet recorded its first single, "Surfin'," for a small, independent company, X Records, as The Pendletones. But unbeknownst to the band, Russ Regan, a promotion man at X's distributor, changed the band's name before the record labels were printed. The Pendletones only learned they were The Beach Boys when they unpacked copies of their first disc.

## 2.7 C. Detroit

In the 1960s, Berry Gordy, Jr.'s Motown Records produced a seemingly endless string of hits by artists such as Martha & The Vandellas, The Supremes, Stevie Wonder, and The Temptations. The label was so successful that its distinctive style became known as the "Motown Sound." The studio where most of the early Motown hits were recorded was called "Hitsville U.S.A.," an old house at 2648 West Grand Boulevard. Designated as a historical site by the state of Michigan, Hitsville U.S.A. is now part of the Motown Historical Museum.

**2.8**  **B. "He's So Fine"**

In 1976, United States District Court Judge Richard Owen ruled that George Harrison had "subconsciously" copied the melody of "He's So Fine" when he penned "My Sweet Lord," which topped the chart in 1970. The action against the former Beatle was initiated in 1971 by Bright Tunes Music, a song publisher that represented the estate of Ronnie Mack, the writer of "He's So Fine" who died shortly after it became a #1 hit for The Chiffons in 1963. Harrison argued that he was not aware of any similarity between the two songs when he wrote "My Sweet Lord," but, in retrospect, he acknowledged their likeness. The court set damages in 1981 at $587,000, the same amount that former Beatles manager Allen Klein had paid for the privilege of suing Harrison when he purchased the rights to "He's So Fine." Clearly annoyed by the proceedings— he wanted to give "My Sweet Lord" to Bright Tunes to settle the case—Harrison wrote "This Song," a sarcastic account of his legal hassles that reached #25 in 1977.

**2.9**  **C. It is the official song of Washington state.**

"Louie Louie" was written in Anaheim by Richard Berry in 1956, but it was popularized by acts from the Pacific Northwest, including Ron Holden And The Playboys, Rockin' Robin Roberts (of The Wailers), and Paul Revere And The Raiders. And even though the song was a hit for The Kingsmen, a Portland, Oregon-based group, "Louie Louie" became closely identified with Washington and the garage-band sound that emerged there in the early 1960s. So after years of lobbying by the song's supporters, Washington state

proclaimed April 12, 1984, to be "Louie Louie" Day.
A subsequent motion to make "Louie Louie" a state song,
however, failed to win approval.

**2.10** **D. "Go Away Little Girl"**
Written by the prolific husband-and-wife team of Gerry
Goffin and Carole King, "Go Away Little Girl," a ditty about
teenage temptation, was twice a #1 tune. On January 12,
1963, pop singer Steve Lawrence's version claimed the top
spot on the *Billboard* Hot 100 for two weeks. Eight years later
on September 11, 1971, teen heartthrob Donny Osmond's
take began a three-week stay at #1. For both artists, "Go Away
Little Girl" was their only chart-topper, although Donny
scored a top single, "One Bad Apple," with four of his brothers
in The Osmonds. Of the other songs in the question, only
Shaun Cassidy's 1977 cover of "Da Doo Ron Ron," which was
a #3 tune for The Crystals in 1963, reached #1.

**2.11** **C. Bill Medley & Bobby Hatfield**
Formed in southern California in 1962, the Righteous
Brothers combined elements of rock 'n' roll with soul music
and, in the process, defined "blue-eyed soul" with #1 hits such
as "You've Lost That Lovin' Feelin'" and "(You're My) Soul
And Inspiration." Medley, the tall baritone, and Hatfield,
the tenor, were not brothers but were called "righteous" by
approving African-American marines who heard the duo
performing at the Black Derby in Santa Ana. Today, "You've
Lost That Lovin' Feelin'" is one of the most played songs on
oldies-style radio.

**2.12** **B. "Suspicion"**
Blessed with an Elvis-like voice, Terry Stafford was cursed by
a series of near misses. His biggest hit, "Suspicion," which
Presley recorded for his 1962 *Pot Luck* album, was released in
February 1964, the month The Beatles debuted in the U.S.

When "Suspicion" peaked at #3 in April, it was a pair
of Beatles tunes—"Can't Buy Me Love" and "Twist And
Shout"—that kept Stafford out of the top spot. Although his
next single reached #25 later that year, subsequent records
failed to chart, and Stafford switched to country music. In
1969 he recorded his composition "Big In Dallas," a few
months before the legendary Buck Owens turned it into a
country classic as "Big In Vegas."

### 2.13 B. J. Frank Wilson & The Cavaliers

"Last Kiss" was written in 1957 by Wayne Cochran, who
based the melodramatic car-crash song on the death of a 16-
year-old friend on her first date. Cochran recorded two versions
of the tune, but both failed to chart. Producer Sonley Roush
later convinced J. Frank Wilson & The Cavaliers to record the
song, which hit #2 on November 7, 1964. Soon after "Last
Kiss" started climbing the charts, Wilson split with The
Cavaliers and, while on tour with his new band in late 1964,
was involved in a head-on collision that killed Roush. In
1974, after "Last Kiss" became a #34 hit for a Canadian group,
Wednesday, Wilson's rendition reached #92. Pearl Jam singer
Eddie Vedder, who was born six weeks after "Last Kiss"
peaked for Wilson in 1964, remembers hearing Wednesday's
cover when he was a boy, but was inspired to record the tune
after he found a copy of Wilson's original at a flea market.

### 2.14 B. Phil Spector

In the early 1960s, seeking to turn a simple pop song into a
three-minute symphony, Spector recorded a multitude of
studio musicians and singers performing simultaneously to
create a lush wall of sound where no single musical element
dominated the song. His orchestrations, which usually
included non-traditional rock instruments such as strings,
horns, and woodwinds, combined with his groundbreaking

use of studio technology—he was a pioneer and ardent proponent of double tracking, the practice of using a track twice (or more) to create a big, full sound—set a new standard in the recording of rock 'n' roll. While the best-known example of the "Wall of Sound" is The Righteous Brothers' 1965 chart-topper "You've Lost That Lovin' Feelin'," it can be heard on many girl-group hits such as The Ronettes' "Be My Baby" and on Ike & Tina Turner's "River Deep, Mountain High," which Spector considered his masterpiece; its relative failure, #88 in 1966, left Spector disillusioned and precipitated his withdrawal from the industry.

**2.15** **A. Roy Orbison topped the chart for the first time.**
Although the 1964 chart-topper "Oh, Pretty Woman" is the song Orbison is best remembered for, "Running Scared" was his first #1 single, peaking on June 5, 1961. A melodramatic lyric about possible rejection, accompanied by a sparse martial rhythm, "Running Scared" was Orbison's third Top 10 tune in a year and reinforced the solitary image he first projected on his 1960 #2 hit, "Only The Lonely (Know How I Feel)." The other three events, including the release of The Beatles' debut American single, "Please Please Me," occurred in 1963.

# The British
# Are Coming
## 1964 and Beyond
. . . . . . . . . . .

O NE HUNDRED and eighty-nine years after Paul Revere's legendary midnight ride, the British again set forth on American shores. This time, though, the attack was led by four saucy lads from Liverpool, armed only with infectious melodies and electric guitars. Within days of landing in New York, the mop tops seized control of the radio stations, stormed the living rooms of a nation, and captured the hearts of a generation. On April 4, 1964, less than two months after the charge began, The Beatles—in an unprecedented and yet unmatched action—secured the top five positions of the *Billboard* Hot 100. The offensive had just begun.

**3.1** The Beatles launched the British Invasion with their first live appearance on the *Ed Sullivan Show* on February 9, 1964. When did the Fab Four next appear on the show?

A. February 16, 1964

B. May 24, 1964

. . . . . . . .
**24**

C. July 12, 1964

D. September 12, 1965

**3.2** **Which group did Ringo Starr play with before joining The Beatles in 1962?**

A. The Quarrymen

B. Rory Storm & The Hurricanes

C. Johnny Kidd & The Pirates

D. The Sunny Siders

**3.3** **Which was the first John Lennon–Paul McCartney composition to appear on the *Billboard* Hot 100?**

A. "Please Please Me" by The Beatles

B. "A World Without Love" by Peter And Gordon

C. "Bad To Me" by Billy J. Kramer With The Dakotas

D. "From Me To You" by Del Shannon

**3.4** **What song won the 1964 Grammy Award for Best Rock & Roll Recording?**

A. "Downtown" by Petula Clark

B. "I Want To Hold Your Hand" by The Beatles

C. "Can't Buy Me Love" by The Beatles

D. "The House Of The Rising Sun" by The Animals

**3.5** **Which Liverpool group topped the British chart first?**

A. The Beatles

B. Gerry And The Pacemakers

C. The Searchers

D. The Swinging Blue Jeans

**3.6** **Who played the "Game Of Love"?**

A. The Monotones

B. Wayne Fontana & The Mindbenders

C. Billy J. Kramer With The Dakotas

D. Freddie & The Dreamers

**3.7** Which group backed The Everly Brothers on their 1966 album, *Two Yanks In England*?

A. Herman's Hermits

B. Dave Clark Five

C. Manfred Mann

D. The Hollies

**3.8** Where did The Beatles play their last concert?

A. Tokyo

B. San Francisco

C. New York

D. Manila

**3.9** Which teenaged singer scored two Top 10 hits with the Spencer Davis Group in 1967?

A. Spencer Davis

B. Steve Winwood

C. Jeff Lynne

D. Rod Stewart

**3.10** What is Long John Baldry best remembered for?

A. He wrote "Long Tall Sally."

B. His first name inspired Elton John's surname.

C. He signed The Beatles to their first recording contract.

D. He was host of BBC-TV's *Top of the Pops*.

**3.11** Which band featuring future Bad Company singer Paul Rodgers and drummer Simon Kirke had a hit with "All Right Now" in 1970?

A. Mountain

B. Deep Purple

C. Free

D. Yes

**3.12** Which British group originally recorded "Without You," a tune that topped the chart for Nilsson in 1972?

A. The Roswells
B. Badfinger
C. Thunderclap Newman
D. The Hollies

**3.13** Which album by a former Beatle featured performances by all of the Fab Four?

A. *All Things Must Pass* by George Harrison
B. *The Concert For Bangla Desh* by George Harrison
C. *Ringo* by Ringo Starr
D. *Rock 'n' Roll* by John Lennon

**3.14** Which statement about The Police is false?

A. The band got its trademark bleached-blonde look when it was hired for a Wrigley's chewing gum advertisement.
B. Drummer Stewart Copeland's father was a CIA agent.
C. "Don't Stand So Close To Me" was inspired by Sting's experiences as a student teacher.
D. "De Do Do Do, De Da Da Da" was the group's first #1 hit in the U.S.

**3.15** Who has scored hits as the lead singer of Ace, Squeeze, and Mike + The Mechanics?

A. Paul Carrack
B. Mike McGear
C. Mike Rutherford
D. Paul Young

# Answers

• • • • • • • • • •

**3.1  A. February 16, 1964**

A week after their *Sullivan* show debut from CBS's Studio 50
(which as the Ed Sullivan Theater is now the home of the *Late
Show with David Letterman*) in New York City, The Beatles
again played on the "big shew." The second show was broadcast live from the Deauville Hotel in Miami. The following
Sunday (February 23) The Beatles appeared a third time, but
this performance had been taped on the afternoon of February
9 before the historic first live show. All three episodes featured
"I Want To Hold Your Hand," which had reached #1 on
the *Billboard* Hot 100 on February 1. The Beatles received
$3,500 for each of the live appearances and $3,000 for the
taped performance.

**3.2  B. Rory Storm & The Hurricanes**

Before replacing Pete Best as The Beatles' drummer,
Richard Starkey pounded the skins for the Liverpool-based
Hurricanes, which he'd joined in 1959. Originally known as
the Raving Texans, Rory Storm's outfit was one of the most
popular local bands. Storm convinced the drummer, who wore
several rings, to adopt "Ringo" as his nickname. In 1960,
The Hurricanes and some other Liverpool groups, including
The Beatles, began playing the nightclub circuit in Hamburg,
Germany, where Ringo became friendly—and occasionally sat
in—with The Beatles. Storm and his group continued to play
after Ringo became a Beatle on August 18, 1962, but never
shared the commercial success that many other Liverpool
bands achieved.

**3.3** D. "From Me To You" by Del Shannon

Following the success of "Runaway," his 1961 chart-topping debut, and "Hats Off To Larry," which hit #5 later the same year, Shannon's career in the U.S. foundered. In Britain, where he continued to churn out Top 10 hits, Shannon was one of the most popular male vocalists. When he toured the U.K. in the spring of 1963, the American singer shared a bill at London's Royal Albert Hall with The Beatles. Shannon, of course, couldn't help but notice the rabid reception the Fab Four received, especially for "From Me To You," the new single that became the group's first British #1 on May 2. But the song, the music of which Paul McCartney said was influenced by "Runaway," failed to register on the *Billboard* Hot 100 after being released in the U.S. on May 27. Meanwhile, Shannon recorded the tune in London before returning to the U.S., where his cover stalled at #77 on July 20, 1963. In 1964, The Beatles re-released "From Me To You" and, as the B-side to a re-released "Please Please Me," it peaked at #41 on April 4.

**3.4** A. "Downtown" by Petula Clark

Although The Beatles dominated the *Billboard* Hot 100 in 1964—six singles occupied the #1 spot for 20 weeks, including an unmatched three back-to-back chart-toppers—it was their compatriot Clark who claimed the 1964 Grammy Award for Best Rock & Roll Recording. A star in Britain during the 1950s and early 1960s, Clark had never charted in the U.S. before "Downtown," which topped the Hot 100 on January 23, 1965, after being released in late 1964. The Beatles were not shut out at the awards ceremony, however. They received Grammies as the Best New Artist of 1964 and, for "A Hard Day's Night," the Best Performance By a Vocal Group.

## 3.5  B. Gerry And The Pacemakers

By the spring of 1963, Beatlemania, which would sweep the U.S. less than a year later, had erupted in Britain. Gerry And The Pacemakers, however, were the first Liverpool band to top the British chart when their debut single, "How Do You Do It?," claimed the #1 spot on April 11, 1963, three weeks before The Beatles moved into first with "From Me To You." The Pacemakers, which became the first British band to lead off with three #1 hits in its homeland, may have embodied the Merseybeat sound better than any other group, including the Fab Four. Although they followed The Beatles across the Atlantic and up the American chart—"Don't Let The Sun Catch You Crying" and "How Do You Do It?" were both U.S. Top 10 hits in 1964—Gerry Marsden's quartet was unable to sustain the pace. "Ferry Cross The Mersey," the 1965 ballad immortalizing the river that flows past Liverpool, was the group's last trip into the Top 10 on either side of the Atlantic.

## 3.6  B. Wayne Fontana & The Mindbenders

The Manchester-based quartet released a handful of singles in Britain—"Um, Um, Um, Um, Um, Um" was a #5 hit there in 1964—before topping the *Billboard* Hot 100 on April 24, 1965, with "Game Of Love," a #2 song in its homeland and the band's first American release. A pair of follow-up singles did not fare particularly well on either side of the Atlantic, and in late 1965 Fontana left the group for a solo career. The Mindbenders, meanwhile, replaced Fontana as vocalist with Eric Stewart and recorded "A Groovy Kind of Love," which became a #2 hit in Britain and the U.S. in 1966. Despite a cameo appearance as the dance band in the 1967 hit movie *To Sir, With Love*, The Mindbenders were unable to repeat their earlier successes and broke up following a couple of uncharted 1968 singles. Stewart and fellow Mindbenders alumnus Graham Gouldman later became members of 10cc.

### 3.7 D. The Hollies

Growing up in the late 1950s, future Hollies Graham Nash and Allan Clarke performed as the Two Teens, patterning themselves after the chart-topping Everly Brothers. Nash and Clarke even waited in the pouring rain after an Everlys' show to get autographs from their mentors. By the spring of 1966 when the Everlys invited The Hollies to accompany them on *Two Yanks In England*, the quintet from Manchester was one of the hottest groups in the country, having cracked the British Top 10 seven times in the previous two-and-a-half years. Nevertheless, none of the 12 tunes on *Two Yanks In England*, eight of which were penned by The Hollies, charted on either side of the Atlantic. While The Everly Brothers were past their prime, The Hollies were about to break through in the U.S. "Bus Stop" and "Stop Stop Stop" entered the American Top 10 later in 1966.

### 3.8 B. San Francisco

The Beatles gave no indication that their show on August 29, 1966, in San Francisco would be their last concert; consequently, more than 16,000 of Candlestick Park's 42,500 seats, which were priced from $4.50 to $6.50, went unsold. The group played for 33 minutes, performing 11 songs, including "I Feel Fine," "Paperback Writer," and "Yesterday," before finishing with "Long Tall Sally." The Beatles' last live public performance took place on January 30, 1969, in London on the roof of the Apple Records building. The impromptu show was filmed for *Let It Be* and lasted about 42 minutes before the police, acting on noise complaints from the neighbors, shut it down. At the end of the last song, "Get Back," John Lennon remarked, "I'd like to say 'thank you' on behalf of the group and ourselves, and I hope we passed the audition."

**3.9** B. Steve Winwood

Spencer Davis included the 15-year-old Winwood when he
formed his Birmingham, England-based, R&B-influenced rock
outfit in 1963. Three years later the Spencer Davis Group
chalked up two #1 songs—"Keep On Running" and
"Somebody Help Me"—in Britain, though neither tune
cracked the American Top 40. In early 1967 "Gimme Some
Lovin'" and "I'm A Man" were Top 10 hits on both sides of the
Atlantic. However, at the height of the quartet's success,
Winwood, whose soulful voice and driving organ defined the
SDG's sound, left the band to form Traffic, a psychedelic-rock
group with which he stayed until 1974. In 1981 Winwood's
second solo album, *Arc Of A Diver*, launched a series of hits for
the singer, including "Roll With It" and "Higher Love," both
of which topped the *Billboard* Hot 100.

**3.10** B. His first name inspired Elton John's surname.

In late 1966 British blues pioneer Long John Baldry hired
Bluesology as his backing band. The group included keyboard
player Reg Dwight, who wrote and sang the outfit's uncharted
1965 debut single, "Come Back, Baby." In 1966, however,
Stuart Brown assumed the lead singer's role, and Baldry's
arrival meant that Dwight became the third-string vocalist.
In the meantime, though, Dwight had met lyricist Bernie
Taupin and had begun plotting a solo career. Dwight played
his last show with Bluesology in Edinburgh in December
1967, and, on the flight home to London, borrowed from
Baldry and Bluesology sax player Elton Dean to fashion a stage
name. On January 10, 1968, Elton John signed his first solo
recording contract.

**3.11  C. Free**

Formed in 1968 in London, Free failed to generate much interest on either side of the Atlantic with its first two albums. Following a 1969 tour of the U.S. opening for Blind Faith, which featured Eric Clapton, the band recorded its third long-player, *Fire And Water*. The album's first single, "All Right Now," written by singer Paul Rodgers and bass player Andy Fraser, peaked at #4 on the *Billboard* Hot 100 on October 17, 1970. After recording four more albums without recapturing the success of "All Right Now," Free dissolved in 1973; shortly thereafter, Rodgers, Free drummer Simon Kirke, and two others incorporated as Bad Company.

**3.12  B. Badfinger**

The quartet from Swansea, Wales, recorded "Without You," a ballad written by guitarist Pete Ham and bassist Tom Evans, for the 1970 album *No Dice*. Originally known as The Iveys, the band was signed to The Beatles' record label, Apple, and its fate was inextricably tied to the Fab Four. Badfinger's first hit, "Come And Get It," which reached #7 on the *Billboard* Hot 100 on April 18, 1970, was written and produced by Paul McCartney. Their biggest single, "Day After Day," was produced by George Harrison, who had used Badfinger on his *All Things Must Pass* and *The Concert For Bangla Desh* albums. On February 5, 1972, two weeks after "Day After Day" peaked at #4, "Without You" topped the chart for Harry Nilsson, an occasional collaborator and longtime drinking buddy of both John Lennon and Ringo Starr.

**3.13**  **C.** *Ringo* **by Ringo Starr**

The Beatles' drummer recruited all three of his former band-
mates to perform on *Ringo*, his 1973 album that yielded three
Top 10 tunes. George Harrison co-wrote and played guitar
on "Photograph," which topped the *Billboard* Hot 100 on
November 24, 1973, making Starr the third member of
the Fab Four to register a #1 hit as a solo performer. Paul
McCartney provided a kazoo-like vocal solo on the album's
second chart-topper, "You're Sixteen," and contributed
instrumental tracks for "Six O'Clock." Harrison and John
Lennon performed on "I'm The Greatest," a Lennon-penned
tune that was inspired by Muhammad Ali. Although the
four Beatles participated in the project, they were never all
in the studio together.

**3.14**  **D. "De Do Do Do, De Da Da Da" was the group's first
#1 hit in the U.S.**

The Police's only American chart-topper was "Every Breath
You Take," a song about a controlling personality that locked
up first place for eight weeks beginning July 9, 1983. "De Do
Do Do, De Da Da Da" was the group's first Top 10 hit, peak-
ing at #10 on the *Billboard* Hot 100 on January 17, 1981.
Less than two years earlier on March 1, 1979, when The Police
began their second American tour at the Whisky A Go Go in
West Hollywood, the band was still virtually unknown. But
following an appearance on March 7 at the Armadillo World
Headquarters in Austin, Texas—advance tickets for the
Wednesday night affair cost $3.00—the group's first single,
"Roxanne," began to get airplay. "We played a little club in
Austin, and the stations started playing the record," Sting told
Joe Smith in *Off The Record*. On April 28, 1979, "Roxanne"
reached #32, and The Police were on their way.

**3.15**  A. **Paul Carrack**

Born in Sheffield, England, Carrack has achieved chart success
with three groups and as a solo performer. As a member of
Ace, the singer scored his first Top 10 hit in 1975 with "How
Long," which peaked at #3 on the *Billboard* Hot 100. After
recording two albums as a keyboardist for Roxy Music, he
vocalized on Squeeze's #49 song, "Tempted," in 1981. Carrack
then teamed with Mike Rutherford of Genesis in 1985 to form
Mike + The Mechanics, which featured Carrack's voice on
three Top 10 hits, including 1989's chart-topping paean to
fathers, "The Living Years." On his own, Carrack sang "Don't
Shed a Tear," a #9 tune in 1988.

• • • • • • • • •

➤ **Hot Track**

On May 26, 1962, "Stranger On The Shore," an instrumental
written and performed by a clarinetist known as Mr. Acker
Bilk, became the first song by a British artist to top the
*Billboard* Hot 100. In the following year Bilk had three
follow-up singles on the chart, but none rose above #59.

➤ **Cool Fact**

The Beatles' first bassist was Stuart Sutcliffe, who befriended
John Lennon when the two were students at the Liverpool
Art College in the late 1950s. On one of the band's trips
to Hamburg in 1960, Sutcliffe fell in love with a German
woman, Astrid Kirchherr. When The Beatles returned to
Liverpool, Sutcliffe remained in Hamburg and enrolled in
art school; Paul McCartney then switched from guitar to bass.
On April 10, 1962, a day before The Beatles were due
to arrive in Hamburg, the 21-year-old Sutcliffe died of a
brain hemorrhage.

# *Game* **B**

## **Rock Around The World Crossword**
• • • • • • •

Although rock 'n' roll began in the U.S., it's now enjoyed worldwide. Solve the puzzle using rock 'n' roll place names. *(Solutions on page 119.)*

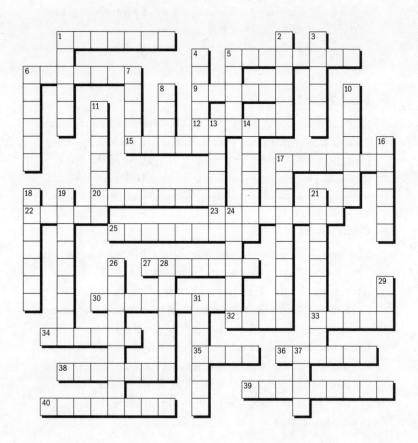

## Across

1. Mitch Ryder And The _____ Wheels
5. Lulu's country
6. Singing Nun's country
9. "North To _____"
12. Neil Young's country
15. Gene Simmons' birthplace
17. _____ Transit Authority
20. "26 Miles (Santa _____)"
22. _____ Mountain Daredevils
23. Del Shannon's state
25. Johnny B. Goode's state
27. Country *Band On The Run* LP recorded in
30. _____ Transfer
32. "Heat Of The Moment" supergroup
33. "Twenty Four Hours From _____"
34. "Country Boy" singer
35. Osmond state
36. The Clash's "_____ Calling"
38. _____ Rhythm Section
39. "_____ Park"
40. The Drifters' street

## Down

1. Bob Dylan's birthplace
2. Paul Anka's birthplace
3. "Spanish _____"
4. Paul Mauriat's country
5. "Never Been To _____"
6. "More Than A Feeling" rockers
7. _____ Sound Machine
8. "Back In The _____"
10. Van Morrison's birthplace
11. Buddy Holly's birthplace
13. "Sweet Home _____"
14. Wings Over _____
16. A-ha's country
17. "Hotel _____"
18. Golden Earring's country
19. "_____ Cats"
21. The Ventures' state
24. "_____ Wants Me"
26. Home of Elvis Presley
28. "The Girl From _____"
29. "Back In The _____"
31. Herb Alpert & The _____ Brass
37. Kent State protest song

# 4

# Peace, Love, and Pop

## The Late Sixties

• • • • • • • • • •

**A**S POLITICAL and social turmoil descended on America, musicians expressed their convictions with thoughtful lyrics set to catchy melodies. It all began on September 20, 1964, when The Beatles ended their second U.S. tour with a performance at New York's Paramount Theater. Watching from the wings was folksinger Bob Dylan who, inspired by their sound, met with John Lennon and Ringo Starr after the show. Ten months later, on July 25, 1965, Dylan shocked the Newport (Rhode Island) Folk Festival audience when he played electric music. "You had the Dylan influence on the lyrics and The Beatles' influence on the music," remembers Al Kooper, a musician who accompanied the singer at Newport, "and a whole new music was born."

**4.1** **What was the original name of The Guess Who?**
A.  The Squires
B.  The Shadows

. . . . . . . .

C. Johnny Kidd & The Pirates

D. Chad Allan & The Expressions

**4.2** "Creeque Alley" is an autobiographical ditty about the formation of The Mamas & The Papas. Where is Creeque Alley?

A. Virgin Islands

B. Saigon

C. Greenwich Village (New York City)

D. New Orleans

**4.3** During its second season (1996–97) on ABC-TV, the *Drew Carey Show*'s theme song was "Five O'Clock World." Which act had a Top 10 hit with this song in 1966?

A. The Vogues

B. The Ventures

C. The Val-Aires

D. The Virtues

**4.4** Who sang lead on the Beach Boys' "Barbara Ann," a #2 hit in 1966?

A. Mike Love

B. Carl Wilson

C. Al Jardine

D. Dean Torrence

**4.5** Which group did Eddie Kendricks, whose solo hits included "Keep On Truckin'" and "Boogie Down," belong to during the 1960s?

A. The Spinners

B. The Four Tops

C. The Miracles

D. The Temptations

**4.6** "You Keep Me Hangin' On," a chart-topping single for The Supremes in 1966, was a Top 10 tune for which act in 1968?

A. Iron Butterfly
B. Kim Wilde
C. Vanilla Fudge
D. Blues Image

**4.7** Who said, "I can't hardly sing, you know what I mean? I'm no Tom Jones, and I couldn't give a [damn]."?

A. Bob Dylan
B. Mick Jagger
C. Ringo Starr
D. Neil Young

**4.8** Which was Blood, Sweat & Tears' highest-charting single?

A. "You've Made Me So Very Happy"
B. "Spinning Wheel"
C. "And When I Die"
D. All of the above

**4.9** In 1969 "Hooked On A Feeling" was a Top 5 hit for which artist?

A. Blue Suede
B. Blue Swede
C. Bobby Goldsboro
D. B.J. Thomas

**4.10** Where did John Lennon and Yoko Ono hold their 1969 bed-in that culminated with the recording of "Give Peace A Chance"?

A. Montreal
B. New York City
C. London
D. Amsterdam

**4.11** Which legendary instrumental group had a 1969 hit with "Hawaii Five-O"?

A. Herb Alpert & The Tijuana Brass

B. The Safaris

C. The Surfaris

D. The Ventures

**4.12** What was the #1 song on July 20, 1969, the day Neil Armstrong first walked on the moon?

A. "In The Year 2525 (Exordium & Terminus)" by Zager & Evans

B. "Bad Moon Rising" by Creedence Clearwater Revival

C. "Good Morning Starshine" by Oliver

D. "Spinning Wheel" by Blood, Sweat & Tears

**4.13** Which act was the first to perform at Woodstock in 1969?

A. Joan Baez

B. Country Joe & The Fish

C. It's A Beautiful Day

D. Richie Havens

**4.14** Who was the lead singer of The Archies?

A. Andy Kim

B. Jeff Barry

C. Ray Stevens

D. Ron Dante

**4.15** Where in California did The Rolling Stones stage their infamous 1969 free concert that was featured in the movie *Gimme Shelter*?

A. Newport

B. Buena Park

C. Altamont

D. Monterey

# Answers

• • • • • • • • • •

**4.1** **D. Chad Allan & The Expressions**

The Winnipeg, Canada-based band that eventually became
The Guess Who was known as Chad Allan & The Expressions
in December 1964 when it recorded its first American hit,
a cover of Johnny Kidd & The Pirates' 1960 British chart-
topper, "Shakin' All Over." Because Canadian radio stations
preferred American and British bands to homegrown ones, the
group's record company concealed the quintet's identity—and
nationality—by printing "Guess Who?" instead of "Chad
Allan & The Expressions" on the single's label. The ruse
worked and on March 22, 1965, "Shakin' All Over" was #1 in
Canada; on July 3 it peaked at #22 on the *Billboard* Hot 100.
The new name proved successful, and as The Guess Who the
band had a string of Top 40 hits, including the 1970 chart-
topper "American Woman."

**4.2** **A. Virgin Islands**

The Mamas & The Papas began in 1964 when John and
Michelle Phillips teamed with Denny Doherty in a folk trio
called The New Journeymen. In the summer of 1965 they
went to the U.S. Virgin Islands, east of Puerto Rico, to
rehearse. Cass Elliot, who was in love with Doherty, soon
followed, rounding out the quartet. For a time the group,
which was supporting itself with cash advances from an
American Express card, lived in tents on a beach on St. John.
When the card reached its spending limit, the foursome found
a gig at Duffy's, a club on Creque's Alley—note the different
spelling—in Charlotte Amalie, the territorial capital on
St. Thomas. "Creeque Alley," John and Michelle Phillips'
chronicle of The Mamas & The Papas' earliest days, reached #5
on June 3, 1967, and was the group's sixth and last Top 5 hit.

### 4.3 A. The Vogues

Although it was neither their first hit nor their biggest, "Five O'Clock World" is The Vogues' most enduring tune. Released on November 27, 1965, just two weeks after their debut single, "You're The One," peaked at #4, "Five O'Clock World" also reached #4 for The Vogues on January 15, 1966. The song, which captures the angst of working for a living, was written for the group by Allen Reynolds, a songwriter who later became Garth Brooks' longtime producer. In 1968 The Vogues had two #7 hits: "Turn Around, Look At Me," a remake of Glen Campbell's 1961 debut single, and "My Special Angel," which was also a #7 tune for Bobby Helms in 1957. The Vogues, a vocal quartet from the Pittsburgh suburb of Turtle Creek, were originally known as The Val-Aires.

### 4.4 D. Dean Torrence

The Beach Boys had befriended Torrence, one-half of Jan & Dean, as early as 1962 when the two bands began appearing on the same concert billings around southern California. In November 1965 as a follow-up to "Help Me, Rhonda," a #1 hit, and "California Girls," a #3 tune, the Beach Boys decided to make *Beach Boys' Party!*, a "live" party album supposedly recorded at Mike Love's house. Taking a break from his own recording session at an adjoining studio, Torrence crashed the "party" and, when asked, suggested the Beach Boys record "Barbara Ann," a tune that Jan & Dean had covered in 1962, a year after it had been a #13 hit for The Regents. For contractual reasons, Torrence's vocals weren't credited on the record, but at the close of the album version of "Barbara Ann," Carl Wilson can be heard saying, "Thank you, Dean."

### 4.5 D. The Temptations

When "Just My Imagination (Running Away With Me)," which featured Eddie Kendricks singing lead, became The Temptations' third #1 single on April 3, 1971, the tenor had parted ways with the Detroit-based quintet. A native of Birmingham, Alabama, Kendricks was singing with The Primes in the Motor City when, in 1961, they merged with The Distants to form The Elgins, an act that would later become The Temptations. The group was one of the most successful hit-makers of the 1960s, enjoying more than 20 Top 40 tunes, including the chart-toppers "My Girl" and "I Can't Get Next To You;" nevertheless, Kendricks chose to venture out alone and was rewarded with a #1 hit of his own when "Keep On Truckin'" parked itself atop the *Billboard* Hot 100 on November 10, 1973. The Temptations were also successful after Kendricks' departure, registering their fourth and final #1 record, "Papa Was a Rolling Stone," on December 2, 1972.

#### 4.6 C. Vanilla Fudge

In the spring of 1967, The Pigeons, a New York–based quartet in search of its big break, recorded "You Keep Me Hangin' On" as a demo disc. For about a year, the band had been playing psychedelic-rock arrangements of Top 40 hits, but the demo of The Supremes' 1966 chart-topper landed the group not only a record deal but also their first single. By then, having been inspired by a friend's passion for a particular flavor of Drumstick-brand ice cream, the band was known as Vanilla Fudge. In July 1967, the debut record reached #67 on the *Billboard* Hot 100; in 1968, however, the single was re-released and on August 31, "You Keep Me Hangin' On" peaked at #6 for Vanilla Fudge. British pop singer Kim Wilde took the tune back to the top of the chart in 1987.

#### 4.7 B. Mick Jagger

The Rolling Stones' frontman admitted his vocal shortcomings in a 1968 interview with *Rolling Stone* magazine when asked a question about his exuberant stage antics. "The Rolling Stones on stage just isn't the Boston Pops Symphony

Orchestra," Jagger explained. "It's a load of noise. On record it can be quite musical, but when you get to the stage it's no virtuoso performance. It's a rock 'n' roll act, a very good one, and nothing more."

**4.8  D. All of the above**

In 1969 Blood, Sweat & Tears popularized jazz-rock: the group's self-titled second album spent seven weeks at #1 on *Billboard*'s pop-album chart, won the 1969 Grammy Award for Album Of The Year, and spawned three million-selling singles, all of which peaked one position shy of the chart's pinnacle. Although BS&T, which prominently featured a horn section in its arrangements, made several more records, it never managed to crack the Top 10 again. The group's early success was undoubtedly due, in part, to James William Guercio, who produced BS&T's 1969 opus and would later collaborate with another horn band, Chicago, on many of that ensemble's biggest hits.

**4.9  D. B.J. Thomas**

"Hooked On A Feeling" hit the Top 10 twice in the United States. Thomas first took the song to the #5 spot on the *Billboard* Hot 100 on January 11, 1969. Then on April 6, 1974, as the first American single for the Swedish septet Blue Swede, it topped the chart. Meanwhile in 1971, British pop impresario Jonathan King—in addition to discovering Genesis and 10cc, he recorded more than 25 singles, including a heavy-metal cover of The Archies' "Sugar, Sugar"—released his own version of "Hooked On A Feeling." Though it didn't chart in the U.S. and only reached #23 in England, King's arrangement included the rhythmic "ooga chuka" chant, which Blue Swede copied. In 1998 "Hooked On A Feeling" enjoyed a brief revival when it accompanied the animated dancing baby that appeared on *Ally McBeal* and the Internet.

### 4.10 A. Montreal

After their marriage in Gibraltar on March 20, 1969, John Lennon and Yoko Ono staged a bed-in for peace on their honeymoon in Amsterdam. The event was so successful generating publicity for peace that the newlyweds decided to hold a second protest in North America. Lennon was barred from entering the U.S., ostensibly for his 1968 drug bust, and when accommodations in the Bahamas were found lacking, Montreal was chosen as the site for the second bed-in. On June 1, Lennon, Ono, and about 40 others, including Tommy Smothers, Petula Clark, and Timothy Leary, recorded "Give Peace A Chance" in Room 1738 of Montreal's Queen Elizabeth Hotel.

### 4.11 D. The Ventures

Perhaps the only thing about the *Hawaii Five-O* TV series (1968–1980) more memorable than Detective Steve McGarrett (Jack Lord) triumphantly ordering his sidekick to "Book 'em, Danno!," is the show's theme song. The Ventures, a quartet from Seattle that boasted a #2 hit with the 1960 guitar-based instrumental classic, "Walk—Don't Run," recorded "Hawaii Five-O" with the help of more than 20 studio musicians, including a horn section. Despite its arresting melody, the song didn't become a hit until it was used in a radio ad for the show; it peaked at #4 on May 10, 1969, as the show's premiere season drew to a close.

### 4.12 A. "In The Year 2525 (Exordium & Terminus)" by Zager & Evans

In the summer of '69, as the world was transfixed by television images of Neil Armstrong and Buzz Aldrin frolicking on the moon's Sea of Tranquillity, American radio waves were inundated by Zager & Evans' "In The Year 2525." Despite the tone of the Rick Evans–penned song, which projects a gloomy view of human existence in future millennia, "In The Year 2525" reached #1 on July 12 and remained at the top of the *Bill-board* Hot 100 for six weeks. But like a walk on the moon, success for the Lincoln, Nebraska-based duo was short-lived: "In The Year 2525" was the first and only single to chart for Zager & Evans.

### 4.13  D. Richie Havens

At 5:07 P.M. on Friday, August 15, 1969, the African-American folksinger from Brooklyn kicked off three days of peace and love at the Woodstock Music and Art Fair in Bethel, N.Y. Although Havens was originally scheduled to play fifth, he was moved to the top of the bill because logistical problems prevented other acts from reaching the concert site. He began his set with a song he co-wrote, "Minstrel From Gault," and followed with a mixture of his own compositions and those of others, including three by The Beatles: "With A Little Help From My Friends," "Hey Jude," and "Strawberry Fields Forever." He did not, however, play the song for which he is best known, "Here Comes the Sun"; in 1971 Havens had his only Top 20 hit with a cover of the George Harrison tune.

### 4.14  D. Ron Dante

The voice of The Archies was 16 years old when he began his professional career in 1961 as a singer-songwriter for Don Kirshner, a New York music publisher. Despite having had a #19 single, "Leader Of The Laundromat"—a spoof of The Shangri-Las' "Leader Of The Pack"—with The Detergents in 1965, Dante was still singing demos and jingles in 1968 when Kirshner started assembling studio musicians and singers for the "band" on the television cartoon show *The Archies*. Although a number of vocalists sang on The Archies' records between 1968 and 1972, Dante was always the group's lead singer. On October 25, 1969, two weeks after "Sugar, Sugar," The Archies' only #1 hit, ended a four-week stay at the top of the chart, he had two songs in the Top 10: "Sugar, Sugar" was #3 and "Tracy," which Dante also sang lead on, peaked at #9 for The Cuff Links. As a jingle singer, Dante worked with a young Barry Manilow and would later serve as producer on many of the pianist's biggest hits, including "Mandy," "I Write The Songs," and "Looks Like We Made It," all of which were chart-toppers.

**4.15  C. Altamont**

On December 6, 1969, an estimated 300,000 people gathered about 40 miles east of San Francisco at Dick Carter's Altamont Speedway in Livermore for a hastily organized free concert featuring The Flying Burrito Brothers, the Jefferson Airplane, and The Rolling Stones. Unfortunately, the peace and music that characterized Woodstock four months earlier deteriorated into mayhem and murder. During the performances, which were captured on film for *Gimme Shelter*, several skirmishes occurred on and near the stage. The Hell's Angels, who were supposed to provide concert security, never gained control of the crowd. Ultimately, as The Rolling Stones finished playing "Under My Thumb," a fight erupted in front of the stage and a Hell's Angels member stabbed Meredith Hunter, an African-American man who had drawn a pistol. Hunter died of his wounds.

# 5

# Love 'em or Hate 'em

## The Seventies

• • • • • • • • • • •

SPARKED BY the increasing commercialization of rock 'n' roll, the 1970s was a decade of constant change. As coffee houses and 45 rpm singles were replaced by larger-capacity sports arenas and more profitable albums, each year brought a new style of music. But whether it was folk-rock or disco, glam or punk, art rock or metal, no single genre dominated rock 'n' roll. So while the 1970s represented some of rock's worst excesses—the *Sgt. Pepper's Lonely Hearts Club Band* movie starring the Bee Gees and Peter Frampton—and such diverse and visceral reactions—punk rising from the ashes of disco—the music of the era remains some of rock 'n' roll's most memorable.

**5.1** Which act professed in song to be an American band?

A. Black Oak Arkansas

B. America

C. Grand Funk

D. Foreigner

**5.2** The Shocking Blue, The Tee Set, and the George Baker Selection all had Top 40 hits in 1970. Which country did these groups come from?

A. Canada

B. Holland

C. Australia

D. France

**5.3** Which artist had a Top 10 hit in 1970 with "Patches," the tale of a ragged 13-year-old Alabama farm boy who becomes the head of the family when his father dies?

A. Clarence Carter

B. Carl Carlton

C. Clarence Clemons

D. Dickey Lee

**5.4** Who wrote "Desiderata," a spoken-word hit in 1971?

A. A lawyer from Terre Haute, Indiana.

B. It is from the Book of Leviticus in the Old Testament.

C. Anonymous. In 1692 the text was found in Old St. Paul's Church, Baltimore.

D. Les Crane, the narrator of the recording.

**5.5** Which three performers comprised the folk-rock act America?

A. Frank Beard, Billy Gibbons, Dusty Hill

B. Guy Gelso, Felix Hanemann, Randy Jackson

C. Danny Hutton, Chuck Negron, Cory Wells

D. Gerry Beckley, Dewey Bunnell, Dan Peek

**5.6** For which pop-rock band did Eric Carmen sing lead vocals before he embarked on a solo career?

A. The Strawbs

B. The Cranberries

C. The Strawberry Alarm Clock

D. The Raspberries

**5.7** Which act did John Fogerty record with following the breakup of Creedence Clearwater Revival?

A. Rockpile

B. The Blue Ridge Rangers

C. The Golliwogs

D. The Bayou Boys


**5.8** Which song was Hamilton, Joe Frank & Reynolds' only #1 hit?

A. "Treat Her Like A Lady"

B. "Don't Pull Your Love"

C. "Fallin' In Love"

D. "Sooner Or Later"


**5.9** In 1976 the Recording Industry Association of America began awarding platinum albums for sales of 1 million copies. Which act received the first platinum album?

A. Iron Butterfly, *In-A-Gadda-Da-Vida*

B. The Eagles, *Their Greatest Hits 1971–1975*

C. Carole King, *Tapestry*

D. Elton John, *Captain Fantastic And The Brown Dirt Cowboy*


**5.10** Which act topped the chart in 1976 with the instrumental "A Fifth Of Beethoven"?

A. Walter Murphy & The Big Apple Band

B. Royal Philharmonic Orchestra

C. Electric Light Orchestra

D. Falco


**5.11** What was Fleetwood Mac's only #1 hit in the U.S.?

A. "Don't Stop"

B. "Go Your Own Way"

C. "Little Lies"

D. "Dreams"

**5.12** Which statement about Harry Chapin is false?

    A. In 1980 "Sequel," the follow-up to "Taxi," charted higher than the original did in 1972.

    B. "Cat's In The Cradle" was a Top 10 hit in 1993 for the pop-metal band Ugly Kid Joe.

    C. Grammy Award–winning country artist Mary Chapin Carpenter is his sister.

    D. He wrote and directed an Academy Award–nominated film.

**5.13** Which song was Peter Frampton's highest-charting single?

    A. "Show Me The Way"

    B. "Baby, I Love Your Way"

    C. "Do You Feel Like We Do"

    D. "I'm In You"

**5.14** How many consecutive #1 singles did the Bee Gees collect from 1977 to 1979?

    A. Four

    B. Five

    C. Six

    D. Seven

**5.15** Which character was not portrayed by the Village People?

    A. Construction worker

    B. Biker

    C. Fire fighter

    D. Cowboy

# Answers

• • • • • • • • • •

**5.1  C. Grand Funk**

Originally known as Grand Funk Railroad, the Flint, Michigan-based hard-rock group proudly declared its heritage in "We're An American Band," a celebration of the notorious and wanton off-stage antics of rock 'n' rollers. The single topped the *Billboard* Hot 100 on July 28, 1973. Ironically, the American band's name was inspired by a Canadian company, the Grand Trunk Railway, a branch line of which extended into Michigan.

**5.2  B. Holland**

A Dutch mini-invasion occurred during the first half of 1970. Leading the charge was The Shocking Blue, which topped the *Billboard* Hot 100 on February 7 with "Venus." Five weeks later on March 14, The Tee Set followed with a #5 hit, "Ma Belle Amie." Then on May 30, "Little Green Bag" peaked at #21 for the George Baker Selection. All three songs had previously been hits in Holland, and an American, Jerry Ross, licensed the songs for release in the United States on his fledgling label, Colossus. Unfortunately for Ross, his source of hits dried up quickly: none of the three groups had another American Top 40 hit until 1976 when "Paloma Blanca" reached #26—albeit on a different label—for the George Baker Selection. In 1986 "Venus" topped the chart for the British vocal group Bananarama.

**5.3  A. Clarence Carter**

A blind R&B singer from Montgomery, Alabama, Carter achieved his greatest chart success with "Patches," which peaked at #4 on the *Billboard* Hot 100 on September 19,

1970. Although the song's main character, Patches, and the singer hail from the same state, it was not Carter, but rather Ronald Dunbar and General Johnson, who wrote the tune. Johnson, the lead singer of the Chairmen Of The Board, had originally recorded "Patches" with his group. Carter's rendition, however, became a hit and later won the 1970 Grammy Award for the Best R&B Song.

**5.4** **A. A lawyer from Terre Haute, Indiana.**
"Desiderata" was penned in 1927 by Max Ehrmann, a lawyer and businessman whose passion was writing poems and plays. After he died in 1945, his widow published "Desiderata" in a book entitled *The Poems of Max Ehrmann*. Eventually, and no one knows exactly how, the poem caught the attention of Frederick Ward Kates, the rector of Baltimore's Old St. Paul's Church. In the late 1950s Kates distributed "Desiderata" to his congregation on parish letterhead, which indicated that the church was founded in 1692. A myth about the poem's creation arose when subsequent reproductions of the work suggested it originated in the 17th century. In 1971 "Desiderata" was a #8 hit for Les Crane, whose previous claim to fame was a four-year marriage to Tina Louise, the actress who played movie star Ginger Grant on *Gilligan's Island*. Crane, a former late-night television talk-show host and radio disc jockey from San Francisco, won the 1971 Grammy Award for Best Spoken Word Recording.

**5.5** **D. Gerry Beckley, Dewey Bunnell, Dan Peek**
The trio, known for Top 10 hits such as "Ventura Highway," "Lonely People," and "Sister Golden Hair," met in the late 1960s while attending high school near London, England, where their fathers were stationed by the U.S. Air Force. After playing around London, the group recorded its first album,

*America*, which was released in late 1971. Written by Bunnell, the band's debut single, "A Horse With No Name," reached #3 in Great Britain. But in the U.S., where America was touring as the opening act for the Everly Brothers, "Horse" topped the *Billboard* Hot 100 on March 25, 1972. America subsequently won the Grammy Award for Best New Artist of 1972.

### 5.6  D. The Raspberries
Eric Carmen, who scored Top 5 hits with "All By Myself," "Hungry Eyes," and "Make Me Lose Control" as a solo artist, apprenticed with The Raspberries during the early 1970s. The Cleveland-based quartet's crisp Beatlesque melodies yielded three Top 20 tunes including the band's biggest hit, "Go All The Way," which peaked at #5 on October 7, 1972. Although The Raspberries' last single, "Overnight Sensation (Hit Record)," reached #18 in 1974, the group disbanded shortly thereafter due to personality conflicts. In 1984 "Almost Paradise," a duet Carmen co-wrote with Dean Pitchford for the movie *Footloose*, was a Top 10 hit for Heart's Ann Wilson and Loverboy's Mike Reno.

### 5.7  B. The Blue Ridge Rangers
After Creedence Clearwater Revival dissolved in 1972, its creative dynamo, John Fogerty, pursued a solo career, single-handedly recording all the instruments and vocals on The Blue Ridge Rangers' self-titled 1973 album. Although Fogerty was a one-man band, the songs he chose, such as George Jones' "She Thinks I Still Care" and Hank Williams' "Jambalaya (On the Bayou)," paid homage to his country and gospel influences. The album yielded two hits—"Jambalaya" peaked at #16 and "Hearts Of Stone" crested at #37.

**5.8** **C. "Fallin' In Love"**

Hamilton, Joe Frank & Reynolds had two Top 10 hits.
On July 17, 1971, "Don't Pull Your Love" reached #4 on
the *Billboard* Hot 100 for the Los Angeles–based threesome
that was comprised of Dan Hamilton, Joe Frank Carollo,
and Tommy Reynolds. In 1972 Reynolds left the group
and was replaced by Alan Dennison. Nevertheless, the new
trio continued to record as Hamilton, Joe Frank & Reynolds,
and on August 23, 1975, "Fallin' In Love" knocked the
Bee Gees and "Jive Talkin'" off the top of the chart. In 1976
the band changed its handle to Hamilton, Joe Frank &
Dennison, but regardless of its name was never able to
match its earlier successes.

**5.9** **B. The Eagles, *Their Greatest Hits 1971–1975***

With five Top 10 hits, including the chart-topping "Best Of
My Love" and "One Of These Nights," *Their Greatest Hits
1971–1975* was released on February 1, 1976, and certified
platinum a mere 23 days later. By the end of 1999 the disc
had sold more than 26 million copies, making it the best-
selling album of the 20th century.

**5.10** **A. Walter Murphy & The Big Apple Band**

A classically trained pianist, Murphy added a disco beat to
Ludwig van Beethoven's "Symphony No. 5 In C Minor" and
on October 9, 1976, almost 150 years after the great composer
died, "A Fifth Of Beethoven" topped the *Billboard* Hot 100.
Shortly after the single was released, Murphy discovered that
another New York–based group was called The Big Apple
Band—it included Nile Rodgers and Bernard Edwards, both
of whom would top the chart in 1978 as members of Chic.
The song was eventually credited to "Walter Murphy" since
he had played most of the instruments. Although his next
single, "Flight '76," an adaptation of Nikolay Rymsky-

Korsakov's "Flight Of The Bumblebee," stalled at #44, Murphy's fortune changed, and undoubtedly increased, when "A Fifth Of Beethoven" was included on the soundtrack of the blockbuster 1977 movie *Saturday Night Fever*.

**5.11 D. "Dreams"**

Fleetwood Mac was one of the late 1970s' premier hit-makers, yet the quintet managed only one chart-topping single— "Dreams," Stevie Nicks' bittersweet ballad about her dissolving personal relationship with bandmate Lindsey Buckingham. Reaching the pinnacle of the *Billboard* Hot 100 on June 18, 1977, "Dreams" was the second single from *Rumours*, the blockbuster album that spent 31 weeks at #1 on the *Billboard* pop-album chart and was ranked by *Billboard* as the top long-player of the decade. Before the group relocated to California and recruited Nicks and Buckingham in 1975, Fleetwood Mac was a British-based blues outfit. In 1969 "Albatross," a guitar instrumental, was a #1 hit in Britain for the band; although the song climbed back to #2 in Britain in 1973, it never charted in the U.S.

**5.12 C. Grammy Award–winning country artist Mary Chapin Carpenter is his sister.**

Despite sharing folk influences and passionate interests in social issues, singer-songwriters Harry Chapin and Mary Chapin Carpenter are not related. While Chapin is his surname, it is her middle name and the first name of her father, who was an executive at *Life* magazine. Harry's father, Jim, was a jazz drummer who played with acts such as Woody Herman and Tommy Dorsey. In 1980 "Sequel" reached #23, one place higher than "Taxi." In 1968 *Legendary Champions*, a film about heavyweight boxers that Harry Chapin wrote and directed, received an Oscar nomination for Best Feature Documentary.

### 5.13  D. "I'm In You"

Surprisingly, Peter Frampton's highest-charting single was from the 1977 follow-up to his best-selling two-record set, *Frampton Comes Alive!*, and not from the blockbuster album itself. Recorded live at Winterland in San Francisco, *Frampton Comes Alive!* occupied the top spot on *Billboard*'s pop-album chart for 10 weeks in 1976 and yielded three hits, "Show Me The Way," "Baby, I Love Your Way," and "Do You Feel Like We Do," which reached #6, #12, and #10 respectively. The next year, however, "I'm In You," a coyly titled ballad from an album of the same name, eclipsed these rankings, peaking at #2 on July 30, 1977. Although Frampton recovered from serious injuries suffered in an automobile accident a year later, he never cracked the Top 10 again.

### 5.14  C. Six

In the late 1970s the Bee Gees dominated the chart like no other act since The Beatles. Beginning December 24, 1977, when "How Deep Is Your Love" topped the *Billboard* Hot 100, the Brothers Gibb reeled off six consecutive #1 hits including "Stayin' Alive," "Night Fever," "Too Much Heaven," "Tragedy," and "Love You Inside Out." Within this streak is another notable achievement. Between "Stayin' Alive"'s four weeks at #1 and "Night Fever"'s eight-week lock on first place, the top spot was occupied by the Bee Gees' younger brother, Andy, with "(Love Is) Thicker Than Water," a tune co-written by Barry, the eldest brother. "Night Fever" was succeeded by "If I Can't Have You," a song the Bee Gees penned for Yvonne Elliman, which meant that Barry Gibb had a hand in writing four back-to-back chart-toppers, breaking John Lennon and Paul McCartney's 1964 mark of three. The Bee Gees' six #1 hits tie the record set by The Beatles for most consecutive chart-toppers by a group.

**5.15**  C. Fire fighter

Through the six characters—a cowboy, an Indian, a construction worker, a G.I., a biker, and a policeman—that made up the group, the Village People established a unique visual identity, something the majority of disco acts were not able to do. Originally intended to appeal to a gay audience, the sextet was conceived in 1977 by French producer-songwriter Jacques Morali, who had seen costumed men dancing at a Greenwich Village disco. And while the gay-themed lyrics resonated with its target market, the group's music gained a mainstream audience. "Y.M.C.A." checked into the #2 spot on the *Billboard* Hot 100 on February 3, 1979, and "In The Navy" sailed into slip #3 later that year on May 19. Not surprisingly, after the success of the latter tune, Alexander Briley, the G.I., added a sailor's suit to his wardrobe.

• • • • • • • • • •

➤ **Hot Track**

"The Long And Winding Road," which reached the top of the *Billboard* Hot 100 on June 13, 1970, was The Beatles' final #1 hit in the U.S. Entering the chart on May 23, six weeks after the group's breakup had become public, the Paul McCartney–penned ballad was the Fab Four's twentieth American chart-topper.

➤ **Cool Fact**

Although the art-rock sound of Yes was popular in the mid-1970s, not everyone was a fan. To avoid any possible confusion between its unadorned three-chord guitar rock and the lavishly orchestrated music of Yes, Bachman-Turner Overdrive named its 1974 album *Not Fragile,* the opposite of *Fragile,* Yes's 1972 hit LP.

# *Game* C

## Duets

• • • • • • •

Match the song to the pair of singers that sang it together.
*(Solutions on page 119.)*

*Song*

1. "Crying"
2. "Mockingbird"
3. "Somethin' Stupid"
4. "Where Is The Love"
5. "You Don't Bring Me Flowers"
6. "Deep Purple"
7. "Mockingbird"
8. "(You're) Having My Baby"
9. "You're The One That I Want"
10. "Endless Love"
11. "Islands In The Stream"
12. "Ebony And Ivory"

*Singer 1*

A. James Taylor
B. Olivia Newton-John
C. Barbra Streisand
D. Nancy Sinatra
E. Charlie Foxx
F. Nino Tempo
G. Roberta Flack
H. Kenny Rogers
I. Odia Coates
J. k.d. lang
K. Lionel Richie
L. Paul McCartney

*Singer 2*

a. Inez Foxx
b. Donny Hathaway
c. Roy Orbison
d. Paul Anka
e. Carly Simon
f. Dolly Parton
g. April Stevens
h. Neil Diamond
i. Frank Sinatra
j. John Travolta
k. Stevie Wonder
l. Diana Ross

. . . . . . . .

# 6

# Small Screens and Drum Machines
## The Eighties
• • • • • • • • • •

TWENTY-FIVE YEARS after television programs such as the *Ed Sullivan Show* and *American Bandstand* first introduced rock 'n' roll to mainstream America, the small screen re-emerged as the single most powerful force shaping pop music. On August 1, 1981, MTV (Music Television) broadcast its first clip, "Video Killed The Radio Star" by The Buggles. Almost overnight, rock was recast as a visual art, and musicians rushed to find a distinctive look. But while the quality of music took a temporary backseat to the performers' appearances, MTV's lasting legacy has been listener-friendly pop music. Ultimately, video didn't kill the radio star, it revitalized the song.

**6.1** Which act had the first #1 hit of the 1980s?
A. Phil Collins
B. KC And The Sunshine Band
C. Stevie Wonder
D. Dolly Parton

• • • • • • • •

**6.2** What was ABBA's last Top 10 hit before the Swedish popsters disbanded in 1982?

A. "Super Trouper"

B. "When All Is Said And Done"

C. "The Winner Takes It All"

D. "Chiquitita"

**6.3** Which act had a Top 10 hit in 1981 with the Roy Orbison classic, "Crying"?

A. Roy Orbison & k.d. lang

B. James Taylor

C. Johnny Rivers

D. Don McLean

**6.4** What was REO Speedwagon named after?

A. A racing car

B. A truck

C. A child's wagon

D. A steam-powered locomotive

**6.5** What was John Cougar Mellencamp's only #1 hit?

A. "Hurts So Good"

B. "Jack & Diane"

C. "R.O.C.K. In The U.S.A."

D. "Small Town"

**6.6** For 10 of 11 weeks during the spring of 1983, Michael Jackson held the #1 spot on *Billboard*'s Hot 100. Which song interrupted Jackson's run?

A. "Mr. Roboto" by Styx

B. "Jeopardy" by the Greg Kihn Band

C. "Come On Eileen" by Dexy's Midnight Runners

D. "Let's Dance" by David Bowie

**6.7** Who played the guitar solo on Michael Jackson's 1983 chart-topper, "Beat It"?

A. Tito Jackson

B. Paul McCartney

C. Eddie Van Halen

D. Joe Walsh

**6.8** Which statement about Bruce Springsteen is false?

A. He once opened for Anne Murray.

B. In 1980 "Hungry Heart" was his first Top 10 hit.

C. Julianne Phillips, his first wife, was the woman he pulled from the crowd in the "Dancing In The Dark" video.

D. The E Street Band, his former backing group, was named after a street in Belmar, New Jersey.

**6.9** Which member of USA for Africa was the first soloist on "We Are The World"?

A. Lionel Richie

B. Michael Jackson

C. Bruce Springsteen

D. Paul Simon

**6.10** Who performed "St. Elmo's Fire (Man In Motion)," the chart-topping title song from the 1985 movie starring Rob Lowe, Emilio Estevez, and Demi Moore?

A. John Parr

B. Richard Marx

C. John Secada

D. Eric Martin

**6.11** What do "Rock Me Amadeus" by Falco, "West End Girls" by the Pet Shop Boys, and "Holding Back The Years" by Simply Red have in common?

A. All were the acts' only Top 20 tune.

B. All were songs that didn't reach the Top 10.

C. All were chart debuts that topped the *Billboard* Hot 100.

D. All were hits that peaked at #2.

**6.12** Who did Vonda Shepard, the *Ally McBeal* songstress, sing a Top 10 duet with in 1987?

A. Aaron Neville

B. James Ingram

C. Teddy Pendergrass

D. Dan Hill

**6.13** What was the Irish band U2 named after?

A. The world's second-highest mountain

B. A pun for "you too" or "you two"

C. An airplane

D. An Irish automobile

**6.14** Which of Milli Vanilli's first four American singles failed to top the *Billboard* Hot 100?

A. "Girl You Know It's True"

B. "Baby Don't Forget My Number"

C. "Girl I'm Gonna Miss You"

D. "Blame It On The Rain"

**6.15** Which statement about Bryan Adams is false?

A. His first charted single was a 1979 disco song.

B. "Heaven" was his first #1 single.

C. His first four #1 singles were all written for movie soundtracks.

D. His middle name is Guy after Guy Fawkes, who tried to assassinate King James I in 1605.

# Answers

●  ●  ●  ●  ●  ●  ●  ●  ●  ●

**6.1  B. KC And The Sunshine Band**

Times change—and so did Harry "KC" Casey and Richard
Finch, the principals of KC And The Sunshine Band. After
racking up four chart-topping disco numbers from 1975 to
1977, Casey and Finch correctly anticipated the decline of
dance music and changed tempo, releasing "Please Don't Go,"
a pure pop ballad that slipped into the top spot of the
*Billboard* Hot 100 on January 5, 1980. "Please Don't Go" was
the last chart appearance for KC And The Sunshine Band,
although KC and Teri DeSario registered a #2 hit eight weeks
later with a duet of Barbara Mason's #5 song from 1965, "Yes,
I'm Ready"; he also scored a solo hit with his last chart entry,
"Give It Up," which reached #18 in 1984.

**6.2  C. "The Winner Takes It All"**

The demise of the Swedish super-group ABBA was
foreshadowed in early 1979 when the decade-long personal
relationship between band members Agnetha and Björn
ended in divorce. Two years later the other couple, Benny and
Anni-Frid, split up. Between the separations, though, ABBA
made their penultimate album of original material, *Super
Trouper*, and on March 14, 1981, the record's first single, "The
Winner Takes It All," peaked at #8 on the *Billboard* Hot 100.
Although ABBA had four more charting singles before
dissolving in late 1982, none of them inched above #27.

**6.3  D. Don McLean**

It took three years and a bit of luck before "Crying" became
a hit for McLean, who covered the Roy Orbison ballad in
1978 for his *Chain Lightning* album. Despite featuring The
Jordanaires, Elvis Presley's longtime backing vocalists, plus a

cast of Nashville's finest session musicians, the record was rejected by McLean's American label. And according to the singer, *Chain Lightning* "bombed" when it was released in Britain. But then in 1980 a disc jockey in Holland began playing "Crying," and the tune topped the Dutch chart, which led to its reissue in Britain where the song also went to #1 on June 21, 1980. Armed with these overseas successes, McLean was able to convince his new American record company to release "Crying." On March 21, 1981, it peaked on the *Billboard* Hot 100 at #5, just three positions shy of the high-water mark set by Orbison's 1961 rendition.

### 6.4 B. A truck

The Champaign, Illinois-based quintet best known for a pair of chart-topping power-pop ballads—1981's "Keep On Loving You" and 1985's "Can't Fight This Feeling"—took its name and logo from a truck called the REO Speedwagon. Founded in 1910 by Ransom Eli Olds, the REO Motor Truck Company of Lansing, Michigan, produced the Speedwagon, a flatbed that could be used for deliveries or equipped to fight fires. Olds began manufacturing vehicles in 1897 when he built cars bearing his name, the Oldsmobiles.

### 6.5 B. "Jack & Diane"

When the pride of Seymour, Indiana, then known only as John Cougar, turned 31 on October 7, 1982, he had a lot to celebrate: "Jack & Diane," his possibly autobiographical ditty about the frustrations of growing up in a small midwestern town, was in the midst of a four-week reign at #1 on *Billboard*'s Hot 100. At the same time, the first single from his chart-topping *American Fool* album, "Hurts So Good," which had spent four weeks in the #2 slot during August, was at #10, giving Cougar two hits in the Top 10 for his birthday.

**6.6** **C. "Come On Eileen" by Dexy's Midnight Runners**
"Billie Jean" stood atop the *Billboard* Top 100 from March 5
to April 22, and "Beat It" from April 30 to May 20. However,
Jackson's attempt at back-to-back #1 singles—a feat accom-
plished by Elvis Presley and The Beatles—was scuttled by
the lively Celtic-soul sound of "Come On Eileen," singer-
songwriter Kevin Rowland's autobiographical tale of a teenaged tryst. Although the Birmingham, England-based band
had scored an earlier #1 hit in Britain—"Geno" on May 3,
1980—"Eileen" was its first and only American hit. The
follow-up single stalled at #86, and the band broke up after
the release of its subsequent album in 1985.

**6.7** **C. Eddie Van Halen**
A hard-rock guitar virtuoso, Van Halen laid down the white-
hot solo on Michael Jackson's "Beat It," the 1983 Grammy
Award's Record Of The Year. Jackson and his producer,
Quincy Jones, asked Van Halen to play the lead part and the
guitarist obliged by providing them with two solos, complete
with his trademark hammer-ons. They used the second
version. The recording session, which also included Toto
members Steve Lukather on bass and rhythm guitar and Jeff
Porcaro playing drums, took place in the fall of 1982 at
Westlake Studios in Los Angeles. Van Halen did not ask to be,
nor was he, paid for his work.

**6.8** **C. Julianne Phillips, his first wife, was the woman he pulled
from the crowd in the "Dancing In The Dark" video.**
An actress, Phillips appeared in the video for "If I'd Been The
One," a #19 song in 1984 for 38 Special. She was not in the
"Dancing In The Dark" clip, which was filmed at the St. Paul
(Minnesota) Civic Center on June 29, 1984, four months
before Phillips met Springsteen after one of his shows in Los

Angeles. The woman Springsteen danced with in the video was Courteney Cox, who is best known for her role as Monica on the NBC-TV series *Friends*. Phillips married Springsteen on May 13, 1985, her twenty-fifth birthday, in Lake Oswego, Oregon, a suburb of Portland where she grew up. The couple's divorce was finalized in 1989.

**6.9   A. Lionel Richie**
Inspired by the success of Band Aid and "Do They Know It's Christmas?," United Support of Artists for Africa came together to raise money to feed the hungry in Africa and the United States. Following the American Music Awards on January 28, 1985, more than 40 entertainers gathered at A&M Studios in Hollywood to record the vocals for "We Are The World" (the instrumental tracks had been laid down beforehand). After Lionel Richie, who co-wrote the song with Michael Jackson, 20 singers performed brief solos in the verses and in the chorus, with the others singing background. "We Are The World" reached the top of the *Billboard* Hot 100 on April 13, 1985, and remained there for four weeks. With sales of eight million singles and four million albums, USA for Africa raised more than $10 million for the less fortunate.

**6.10   A. John Parr**
A British-born singer-songwriter, Parr was recruited to sing "St. Elmo's Fire (Man In Motion)" by David Foster, the producer of the movie soundtrack. Parr and Foster also teamed up to write the song, which was inspired by Foster's fellow Canadian, Rick Hansen, the Man in Motion who spent more than two years pushing his wheelchair 25,000 miles around the world to successfully raise awareness of, and funding for, spinal cord injury research. "St. Elmo's Fire (Man In Motion)" reached the top of the *Billboard* Hot 100 on September 7, 1985, and stayed there for two weeks. Although Parr released

his second album in 1986 and his songs were included on several other soundtracks, his star never burned as brightly as on "St. Elmo's Fire."

**6.11** **C. All were chart debuts that topped the *Billboard* Hot 100.**
Falco's "Rock Me Amadeus" reached #1 on March 29, 1986. Six weeks later on May 10, "West End Girls" and the Pet Shop Boys claimed the top spot. And on July 12, Simply Red scored its first #1 with "Holding Back The Years." All of the acts had another Top 20 song: in 1986 "Vienna Calling" hit #18 for Falco, the Pet Shop Boys and Dusty Springfield earned a #2 in 1987 with "What Have I Done To Deserve This?", and in 1989 a cover of "If You Don't Know Me By Now" returned Simply Red to the top of the list.

**6.12** **D. Dan Hill**
A Canadian-born balladeer, Hill had a #3 hit with 1977's "Sometimes When We Touch," which he wrote with the prolific tunesmith Barry Mann. A decade later Hill and Shepard reached #6 with "Can't We Try," a song Hill composed with his wife, Bev. Since "Can't We Try," Hill has focused on his songwriting, penning tunes for the likes of Celine Dion and country singers Sammy Kershaw and Mark Wills. Shepard, meanwhile, recorded three albums that went largely unnoticed by the public. Then, while performing in a Los Angeles nightclub, she was spotted by TV producer David E. Kelley and cast as the chanteuse on *Ally McBeal*. "Searchin' My Soul," which originally appeared on Shepard's 1992 album, is the TV show's theme song.

**6.13** **C. An airplane**
On May 1, 1960, an American U-2 spy plane and its pilot, Gary Powers, were shot down while flying a high-altitude mission over the former Soviet Union. The U-2 Incident, as it

became known, heightened tensions in the Cold War between the Americans and the Soviets and briefly made the U-2 the most famous plane in the world. In 1978 Adam Clayton, the bass player and manager of The Hype, approached a friend's brother, Steve Averill, for some advice about the music business. During their discussions, Clayton said that he'd like a new moniker for the group, something intriguing but ambiguous, like XTC. Averill, a rock singer and a graphic artist—he would later design the cover of the band's *Boy* album—suggested U2, which embodied the intrigue of the Cold War and, because it was also the name of a submarine and a battery, had a nebulous feel to it.

**6.14** **A. "Girl You Know It's True"**
Milli Vanilli's Rob Pilatus and Fabrice Morvan were not nearly as convincing in their lip-synching roles as producer Frank Farian's carefully constructed Eurodisco was to record buyers. Before being exposed as a fraud, Milli Vanilli released five singles in the U.S.: although the group's debut single, "Girl You Know It's True," peaked at #2—on April Fools' Day, 1989—the next three, "Baby Don't Forget My Number," "Girl I'm Gonna Miss You," and "Blame It On The Rain," topped the chart. The fifth single, "All Or Nothing," reached #4 in early 1990. On November 14, 1990, less than a year after Milli Vanilli's last chart-topper, Farian confirmed that Pilatus and Morvan had not sung on the group's records; five days later, the National Academy of Recording Arts and Sciences rescinded Milli Vanilli's 1989 Grammy Award for Best New Artist.

**6.15** **A. His first charted single was a 1979 disco song.**
Bryan Adams' first solo single, "Let Me Take You Dancing," failed to crack the *Billboard* Hot 100, even though it sold 240,000 copies during the summer of 1979 when it was one

of the most popular tunes in New York City dance clubs. One of the first numbers Adams and his former collaborator Jim Vallance wrote together in 1978, "Let Me Take You Dancing" was originally recorded as a rock 'n' roll tune, but the track was remixed and sped up, giving it a disco beat and making Adams' voice sound, he said, "like a chipmunk." In 1976 Adams' first chart appearance was as a member of Sweeney Todd, a Vancouver-based pop band that had scored a #1 hit in Canada with "Roxy Roller." After Nick Gilder, the group's original lead singer, quit, the 16-year-old Adams re-recorded the vocals on "Roxy Roller"; his version of the song reached #99 in its only week on the Hot 100.

● ● ● ● ● ● ● ● ● ●

## ➤ Hot Track

Released in late 1983, Cyndi Lauper's *She's So Unusual* became the first debut album of the rock era to yield four Top 10 singles. Following her breakout hit, the #2 *Girls Just Want To Have Fun,* Lauper topped the *Billboard* Hot 100 with *Time After Time.* Her next two releases, *She Bop* and *All Through The Night,* peaked at #3 and #5, respectively. For her efforts, Lauper was honored as the Best New Artist at the 1984 Grammy Awards.

## ➤ Cool Fact

Unlike a phonograph record, the music on a compact disc is played from the inside out.

# Words and
#         Music By
## The Songwriters
• • • • • • • • • •

**W**HILE THE artists performing songs invariably get the glory, the songwriters are the unsung heroes of rock 'n' roll. The work they do—cleverly weaving a catchy melody around a well-crafted lyric—is usually long and arduous, filled with self-doubt, and a test of discipline. There is no set formula for creating a song: sometimes the music comes first, sometimes the words; but rarely do the two arrive together. And although a hit tune can earn lots of money for the composer, financial gain is not the main motivation. Rather, songwriters hope for something much less tangible—to create a memorable song that makes people smile.

**7.1** **What inspired Otis Blackwell to write "All Shook Up"?**

A. A well-shaken bottle of Coca-Cola

B. An earthquake

C. A New York City taxi ride

D. The song "Shake, Rattle & Roll"

. . . . . . . .

**7.2** Which songwriting team wrote such #1 hits as "Wake Up Little Susie," "All I Have To Do Is Dream," and "Bird Dog" for the Everly Brothers?

A. Jeff Barry & Ellie Greenwich

B. Felice Bryant & Boudleaux Bryant

C. Jerry Leiber & Mike Stoller

D. Roy Acuff & Fred Rose

**7.3** Where is the Brill Building located?

A. New York City

B. Memphis

C. Detroit

D. Nashville

**7.4** Which song did Beach Boy Brian Wilson borrow the melody for "Surfin' U.S.A." from?

A. "Twistin' U.S.A."

B. "Palisades Park"

C. "Sweet Little Sixteen"

D. "Back In The U.S.A."

**7.5** Who wrote "My Guy" by Mary Wells and co-wrote "My Girl" by The Temptations?

A. Stevie Wonder

B. Smokey Robinson

C. Berry Gordy, Jr.

D. Marvin Gaye

**7.6** Which of the following Top 40 hits was not written by Bob Dylan?

A. "All Along the Watchtower" by Jimi Hendrix

B. "Mighty Quinn (Quinn The Eskimo)" by Manfred Mann

C. "Turn! Turn! Turn! (To Everything There Is A Season)" by The Byrds

D. "If Not For You" by Olivia Newton-John

**7.7** How old was Janis Ian when she wrote her #14 hit, 1967's "Society's Child (Baby I've Been Thinking)"?

A. 14
B. 16
C. 17
D. 19

**7.8** Which Top 10 tune inspired Chip Taylor to write "Angel Of The Morning"?

A. "Ruby Tuesday" by The Rolling Stones
B. "Young Girl" by The Union Gap Featuring Gary Puckett
C. "Younger Girl" by The Critters
D. "Mrs. Robinson" by Simon & Garfunkel

**7.9** Which act did Jimmy Webb originally write "MacArthur Park" for?

A. Richard Harris
B. Marvin Gaye & Tammi Terrell
C. The Association
D. Procol Harum

**7.10** What inspired the name of John Lennon's central character, "old flattop," in The Beatles' 1969 chart-topper "Come Together"?

A. A character from a Chuck Berry song.
B. The model name of his favorite guitar.
C. A villain from the *Dick Tracy* cartoon strip.
D. Elvis Presley's army haircut.

**7.11** Who wrote "Chelsea Morning," the song after which Bill and Hillary Rodham Clinton named their daughter?

A. Mimi Farina
B. Joan Baez
C. Judy Collins
D. Joni Mitchell

**7.12** Who wrote "A Boy Named Sue," "The Unicorn," and
"The Cover of *Rolling Stone*"?
A. Shel Silverstein
B. Jerry Reed
C. Ray Stevens
D. Jim Stafford

**7.13** Who wrote Captain and Tennille's first hit,
"Love Will Keep Us Together"?
A. Jasper Westhampton
B. Burt Bacharach & Hal David
C. Neil Sedaka & Howard Greenfield
D. Neil Diamond

**7.14** Which movie motivated Bob Seger to write his #4 tune,
"Night Moves"?
A. *American Graffiti*
B. *The Graduate*
C. *In Praise of Older Women*
D. *Summer of '42*

**7.15** Who co-wrote "Dum Dum" by Brenda Lee, "Put A Little Love
In Your Heart" by Jackie DeShannon, and "Bette Davis Eyes"
by Kim Carnes, all of which were Top 10 hits?
A. Burt Bacharach & Hal David
B. Neil Diamond
C. P.F. Sloan
D. Jackie DeShannon

# Answers

• • • • • • • • • •

**7.1 A. A well-shaken bottle of Coca-Cola**
In 1956 thanks largely to the success of "Don't Be Cruel,"
the #1 tune he penned for Elvis Presley, Otis Blackwell was
working as a writer for Shalimar Music, a New York song
publisher. Al Stanton, a colleague, "shook the Coke bottle 'til
it fizzed over and dared me to write something about that,"
Blackwell told Tom Russell in 1987 for the book *And Then I
Wrote*. The tunesmith responded with "All Shook Up," which
Presley took to the top of the chart for nine weeks during the
spring of 1957. Although Blackwell authored the song by
himself, Colonel Tom Parker, Presley's manager, would not
allow his client to record any song until the composer agreed
to split the writing credit—and the royalties—with the
singer. As with "Don't Be Cruel," Blackwell and Presley
shared the profits and the credit for "All Shook Up."

**7.2 B. Felice Bryant & Boudleaux Bryant**
Several years before Phil and Don Everly took the Bryants'
"Bye Bye Love" to #2 in 1957, Boudleaux's barber told him
that the Everly boys could sing, but the songwriter dismissed
his haircutter's words as those of a hopeful father. After the
surprising success of "Bye Bye Love," however, the Bryants, a
husband-and-wife team with several country hits to their
credit, began crafting tunes especially suited for the Everlys'
two-part harmonies. In addition to the three chart-toppers,
the Bryants contributed several other hits, including
"Problems"—a #2 song in 1958—to the Everlys. Although
the Everly Brothers were proficient songsmiths (they penned
the chart-topping "Cathy's Clown" and other Top 10 tunes),
Don Everly said in 1987, the year Boudleaux died, "If it wasn't
(sic) for the Bryants, the Everly Brothers wouldn't be here."

**7.3** **A. New York City**

The Brill Building, which is located at 1619 Broadway, was home to a group of songwriters that created many of the most popular hits of the 1960s. Completed at the depths of the Depression in 1931, the building and its low rents were attractive to music publishers who housed dozens of aspiring tunesmiths in its offices. When the "Brill Building sound"— carefully crafted pop songs by writers such as Barry Mann, Carole King, and Neil Sedaka that were meticulously recorded by producers like Phil Spector—was at its zenith in the early 1960s, more than 150 music-related businesses inhabited 1619 Broadway and the neighboring properties, 1650 and 1697. The rise of acts in the mid-1960s that performed their own compositions, such as The Beatles and Bob Dylan, led to the end of the Brill Building era.

**7.4** **C. "Sweet Little Sixteen"**

Like many of rock 'n' roll's finest songwriters, including John Lennon, Keith Richards, and Bruce Springsteen, Brian Wilson was influenced by the music of Chuck Berry. In his autobiography, *Wouldn't It Be Nice*, Wilson recalls that when composing "Surfin' Safari," he was "trying to play the piano the way Chuck Berry played his guitar." Wilson also acknowledges the influence of Berry, as well as that of "Twistin' U.S.A." by both Danny & The Juniors and Chubby Checker, on "Surfin' U.S.A.," which became The Beach Boys' first Top 10 hit when it crested at #3 on May 25, 1963. Berry, however, thought that Wilson had copied the surf song's melody from "Sweet Little Sixteen," a #2 tune for Berry in 1958. After Berry voiced his claim to Murry Wilson, Brian's father and The Beach Boys' manager, the elder Wilson assigned the "Surfin' U.S.A." copyright to Berry. For reasons unknown to Brian, the assignment included the rights to, and royalties for, the lyrics, which were written by Brian, not Berry.

**7.5  B. Smokey Robinson**

His first co-writing credit was "Got A Job," an uncharted number recorded by The Miracles in response to The Silhouettes' 1958 #1 hit, "Get A Job," so it's fitting that Robinson was involved in writing the chart-topping "My Guy" and its "answer" song, "My Girl." Robinson had established himself as a writer when "Shop Around," which he co-wrote and recorded with The Miracles, peaked at #2 on the *Billboard* Hot 100 on February 20, 1961, becoming the first Motown pop hit. Writing for Mary Wells, he registered three Top 10 hits before "My Guy" became, on May 16, 1964, the first Motown single to top the pop chart. Less than a year later on March 6, 1965, The Temptations went to #1 with "My Girl," which Robinson co-wrote. In addition to the many hits he wrote and recorded with The Miracles—"The Tears Of A Clown" topped the chart on December 12, 1970—Robinson's songs have been recorded by artists inside Motown and out, including The Beatles who covered "You Really Got A Hold On Me" in 1963.

**7.6  C. "Turn! Turn! Turn! (To Everything There Is A Season)"
by The Byrds**

The music for "Turn! Turn! Turn!" was written by folk-music legend Pete Seeger, who adapted the lyrics from the Old Testament's Book of Ecclesiastes 3:1–3:8. On December 4, 1965, the tune became a #1 hit for The Byrds, a pioneering folk-rock quintet based in Los Angeles. "Turn! Turn! Turn!" has the distinction of being the #1 single with the oldest lyrics.

**7.7  A. 14**

Growing up in East Orange, New Jersey, Janis Ian witnessed the bigotry that she depicts in "Society's Child (Baby I've Been Thinking)," her poignant account of an interracial teen romance that eventually drowns in intolerance. When the song peaked at #14 on the *Billboard* Hot 100 on July 15, 1967, a few months after her sixteenth birthday, the singer found herself in the middle of the highly charged racial debate taking place in America during the 1960s. "There were a lot of threats from 'Society's Child,'" she told Paul Zollo in *Songwriters On Songwriting*. "A lot of bomb threats. There were whole areas of the country that I couldn't tour in." Ian retired temporarily from the music business because of the pressure. She returned, and in 1975 scored a #3 hit with "At Seventeen," an introspective tune that earned her a Grammy Award for Best Pop Vocal Performance, Female.

**7.8 A. "Ruby Tuesday" by The Rolling Stones**
Although Chip Taylor considers himself a country singer-songwriter, his best-known tunes are pop songs, including "Wild Thing," a 1966 chart-topper for The Troggs, and "Angel Of The Morning," which has twice been a Top 10 hit. In the mid-1960s Taylor was working with Evie Sands, a young blue-eyed soul singer from Brooklyn. "I wrote 'Angel Of The Morning' after hearing The Rolling Stones' song 'Ruby Tuesday' on the car radio when I was driving into New York City," the Yonkers-born tunesmith remembered in 1997. "I wanted to capture that kind of passion." Sands recorded "Angel" in 1967, but before the disc could take flight, her record company went out of business. The next year Merrilee Rush & The Turnabouts took the tune to #7 on the *Billboard* Hot 100, and in 1981 "Angel" landed at #4 for Juice Newton.

**7.9 C. The Association**
Jimmy Webb and producer Bones Howe had worked together on The 5th Dimension's "Up—Up And Away," a tune that Webb wrote. Howe's next project was producing The Association and he mentioned to Webb that he was looking for a long rock piece with, perhaps, a classical feel to it. Webb found inspiration in Los Angeles' MacArthur Park, which he

often visited with his girlfriend, who worked across the street from it. Unfortunately, when Webb presented the song to The Association, the band hated it. Sometime later, however, he played the piece for Irish actor Richard Harris, who had established himself as a singer in the role of King Arthur in the 1967 movie musical *Camelot*. Harris recorded "MacArthur Park," which climbed to #2 on June 22, 1968, and eight more of Webb's thematically related songs, for his *A Tramp Shining* concept album.

**7.10  A. A character from a Chuck Berry song.**

The automobile is one of Berry's recurring lyrical themes, and in his 1955 song "You Can't Catch Me," the songwriter recounts a late-night drag race on the New Jersey Turnpike between himself and a crew-cut challenger he dubs "flattop." The Beatles were big fans of Berry, performing and recording several of his tunes, including "Roll Over Beethoven" and "Rock & Roll Music." In "Come Together"'s stream-of-consciousness lyric, John Lennon pays homage to Berry and "flattop," who by 1969 had very long hair. After "Come Together" became a hit, Berry, always a jealous guardian of his copyright, reportedly questioned Lennon about not crediting him for his contribution to the Fab Four's chart-topper. According to legend, the Beatle asked Berry what he thought the song was worth and then wrote the rock 'n' roll pioneer a check for the figure he named.

**7.11  D. Joni Mitchell**

"Chelsea Morning," a sunny melody about being in love in a bustling city, was written by Mitchell, reportedly while she was living at 41 West 16th Street in New York City's Chelsea neighborhood in 1967. The song subsequently appeared on her 1969 album, *Clouds*. But it is Judy Collins' rendition of the tune, which peaked at #78 in August 1969, that influenced the naming of the former First Daughter. Collins, who scored a Top 10 hit in 1968 with another Mitchell composition, "Both Sides Now," is a favorite singer of the Clintons. On January 20, 1993, Collins performed "Chelsea Morning" at the President's Inaugural Gala.

**7.12  A. Shel Silverstein**
Perhaps most familiar as the author and illustrator of best-selling children's books or as a cartoonist and humorist for *Playboy*, Silverstein was also a prolific songwriter. In addition to the three songs in the question, all of which were Top 10 hits, Silverstein penned hundreds of songs that have been covered by artists as diverse as Marlo Thomas and Marilyn Manson. In 1969 "A Boy Named Sue" garnered Silverstein a Grammy Award for Best Country Song. Silverstein also recorded more than a dozen albums, including *Where The Sidewalk Ends*, the winner of the 1984 Grammy Award for the Best Recording For Children.

**7.13  C. Neil Sedaka & Howard Greenfield**
Sedaka included "Love Will Keep Us Together" on his 1974 album, *Sedaka's Back*, which was released as Captain and Tennille were recording their first long-player. An executive at the duo's record company heard Sedaka's version and played it for the husband-and-wife team, who immediately recognized its hit potential. On June 21, 1975, their cover of "Love Will Keep Us Together" began a four-week stay at #1; it later won the Grammy Award for Record Of The Year. As a tribute to the song's writer, Captain and Tennille included the phrase, "Sedaka is back," among the "da, da, das" in the song's fade out.

**7.14**  A. *American Graffiti*

As teenagers growing up in Ann Arbor, Michigan, Bob Seger and his friends held parties, called "grassers," in the outlying farm fields. In 1964, when he was 19 years old, Seger began a passionate year-long relationship with a dark-haired Italian-American woman. But it wasn't until he saw George Lucas's 1973 coming-of-age movie that Seger thought to incorporate these pieces of his youth into a song. "Night Moves" was inspired by *American Graffiti*, he told the authors of *Behind The Hits*. "I came out of the theater thinking, 'Hey, I've got a story to tell, too.'" Near the end of the song, Seger mentions the music of 1962, an apparent reference to the movie, which was set in that year. "Night Moves," the first Top 10 hit for Bob Seger & The Silver Bullet Band, peaked at #4 on the *Billboard* Hot 100 on March 12, 1977.

**7.15**  D. Jackie DeShannon

A woman of many talents, DeShannon has had success as a singer, songwriter, and actress. In 1965, the year after she opened for The Beatles on their American tour, DeShannon scored a #7 hit with Burt Bacharach and Hal David's "What The World Needs Now Is Love"; she registered her highest chart position, #4, in 1969 with "Put A Little Love In Your Heart," a tune she co-wrote. During the mid-1960s DeShannon had principal roles in a few teen movies, including 1967's *C'mon, Let's Live A Little*, which featured Kim Carnes in a supporting role. It was Carnes, of course, who re-interpreted DeShannon's 1975 version of "Bette Davis Eyes," sending it to the top of the *Billboard* Hot 100 for nine weeks beginning May 16, 1981. "Bette Davis Eyes" earned DeShannon and her collaborator Donna Weiss the 1981 Grammy Award for Song Of The Year.

# Shooting Stars
## The One-Hit Wonders

• • • • • • • • • •

**H**ERE TODAY, gone forever. For a brief, shining moment, the one-hit wonders soar to the top of the chart before rapidly disappearing into the musical abyss from which they came. Understanding why their success is so fleeting is as difficult as explaining what makes a hit record in the first place. But no matter how quick and complete their fall from glory, the one-hit wonders have succeeded where countless others have failed. And while it might be easy to write off these one-trick ponies as mere flashes in the pan, their music is an essential part of the rock 'n' roll soundtrack.

**8.1** Who had his only Top 40 pop hit with "Blue Suede Shoes" in 1956?

A. Duane Eddy

B. Carl Perkins

C. Ronnie Hawkins

D. Gene Vincent

**8.2** Which so-called one-hit wonder actually had three other Top 40 hits, including "Tonight I Fell In Love," a #15 song in 1961?

A. Maurice Williams & The Zodiacs
B. The Tokens
C. Hollywood Argyles
D. Ernie K-Doe

**8.3** Which song was a #1 hit for Lorne Greene, who is best known as Ben Cartwright on the 1960s television show *Bonanza*?

A. "Ballad Of The Green Berets"
B. "Big Bad John"
C. "Honeycomb"
D. "Ringo"

**8.4** For which act was "I Fought The Law" a Top 10 hit in 1966?

A. The Standells
B. The Prisonaires
C. Bobby Fuller Four
D. The Gentrys

**8.5** Which 1966 song was Bobby Hebb's only Top 20 hit?

A. "Sunny"
B. "Sunny Afternoon"
C. "Sunshine"
D. "Sunshine Superman"

**8.6** Which pop act had a Top 10 hit in 1968 with "I Wonder What She's Doing Tonite"?

A. Tommy Boyce & Bobby Hart
B. The American Breed
C. Jay & The Americans
D. The Lemon Pipers

**8.7** Which 1968 one-hit wonder included Tommy Chong, one-half of the 1970s comedy duo Cheech and Chong?
A. Little Caesar & The Consols
B. Little Anthony & The Imperials
C. Bobby Taylor & The Vancouvers
D. Johnnie Taylor & The Five Echoes

**8.8** Which group scored a #2 hit in 1970 with "The Rapper"?
A. Five Man Electrical Band
B. Sailcat
C. The Jaggerz
D. Alive And Kicking

**8.9** Which song was a #2 hit in 1970 for The Poppy Family?
A. "Seasons In The Sun"
B. "O-o-h Child"
C. "Stay Awhile"
D. "Which Way You Goin' Billy?"

**8.10** Which group's only hit was "Precious And Few"?
A. Apollo 100
B. Climax
C. Malo
D. Sailcat

**8.11** Who sang the Top 10 hit "Good Time Charlie's Got The Blues" in 1972?
A. Cliff DeYoung
B. Danny O'Keefe
C. Dave Loggins
D. Daniel Moore

**8.12** Which group had a #1 hit in 1973 with "Brother Louie"?

A. The Mammy Blues
B. The Kingsmen
C. The Left Banke
D. Stories

**8.13** What was George McCrae's 1974 hit?

A. "Rockin' Chair"
B. "Rock Your Baby"
C. "Rock Me Gently"
D. "Rock The Boat"

**8.14** Which disco act cracked the Top 20 with "Don't Let Me Be Misunderstood," a 1965 hit for The Animals?

A. Parliament
B. Silver Convention
C. Santa Esmeralda
D. Con Funk Shun

**8.15** Which act had a 1987 chart-topper with "At This Moment"?

A. Johnny & The Distractions
B. Tommy Tutone
C. Henry Lee Summer
D. Billy Vera & The Beaters

# Answers

. . . . . . . . . . .

**8.1** **B. Carl Perkins**
Beginning May 19, 1956, "Blue Suede Shoes" spent four
weeks at #2, and although it was his only song to rise above
#67 on the pop chart, Perkins is nevertheless regarded as a
rock 'n' roll pioneer. Born into Depression-era poverty in
northwestern Tennessee, he learned to play guitar listening
to Grand Ole Opry radio broadcasts and watching his guitar-
playing neighbor, a black sharecropper. Perkins blended
country and R&B into the rockabilly sound of "Blue Suede
Shoes," which became Sun Records' first million-seller.
Unable to follow up his pop-chart success—he did have some
country hits—while contemporaries such as Elvis Presley and
Jerry Lee Lewis became stars, Perkins slipped into alcoholism
and eventually quit performing. He returned to the stage in
1964 and, at the end of a well-received British tour that year,
Perkins' reputation as a rock legend was cemented when The
Beatles invited him to the Abbey Road studios to watch them
record two tunes from his 1957 *Dance Album*, "Matchbox"
and "Honey Don't."

**8.2** **B. The Tokens**
The success of The Tokens' second charted single quickly
erased the group's first hit from the collective memory: seven
months after "Tonight I Fell In Love" reached a respectable
#15 on the *Billboard* Hot 100, the quartet released "The Lion
Sleeps Tonight," which topped the chart on December 18,
1961. Although The Tokens continued to record, their next
Top 40 hits would be years away; in 1966 "I Hear Trumpets
Blow" peaked at #30 and the next year "Portrait Of My Love"
reached #36. The members of the group had spent the inter-
vening period working as producers for other acts, most

. . . . . . . . . . . . . . . .

notably The Chiffons, who scored a #1 hit with the Tokens-produced "He's So Fine." In 1994 "The Lion Sleeps Tonight," which was included on *The Lion King* movie soundtrack, re-charted and reached #51 for The Tokens.

### 8.3 D. "Ringo"

In 1964 *Bonanza* was a top-rated television show on NBC, and the show's stars made a number of records. One of the songs on the second cast album, *Welcome To The Ponderosa*, was the tale of a gun-slinging outlaw, Ringo, whose life was saved by Lorne Greene's character, the sheriff. Years later, when the two confront each other, Ringo wins the draw, but the outlaw spares the law man's life. Greene, who had been a radio announcer in his native Canada during World War II, spoke the words of "Ringo," which reached #1 on December 5, 1964. Greene's only other charting single, a follow-up to "Ringo," stalled at #72 in early 1965.

### 8.4 C. Bobby Fuller Four

Founded in El Paso, Texas, where they had released a few local singles in the early 1960s, the Bobby Fuller Four achieved their greatest successes after moving to California in 1964. Upon hearing the driving surf-guitar of Dick Dale & The Del-Tones, the BF4 flirted with their own brand of surf music but the band soon returned to its Texan roots, adopting a Buddy Holly–influenced sound. Not coincidentally, both of the band's charted singles are Holly related. The now-classic "I Fought The Law" was written by Sonny Curtis, who became the lead singer of The Crickets after Holly died, and hit #9 on the *Billboard* Hot 100 on March 12, 1966. Two months later, on May 14, the soon-forgotten cover of Holly's "Love's Made A Fool Of You" peaked at #26. On July 18, 1966, Bobby Fuller's bloodied body was found soaked in gasoline in his mother's Oldsmobile; although his death was ruled a suicide, many of the singer's friends believe he was murdered.

**8.5 A. "Sunny"**

Bobby Hebb's recording career can be summed up in one word: "Sunny." According to BMI, an agency that monitors the public performance of music, "Sunny" is one of the most-played songs ever, having been broadcast more than 5 million times since 1966. During the summer of 1966, when Hebb was an opening act on The Beatles' last American tour, "Sunny" peaked at #2 on the *Billboard* Hot 100. However, after the follow-ups to "Sunny" stalled at #39 and #84, Hebb disappeared from the pop chart. Nevertheless, he still performs occasionally around Boston, his home since the mid-1970s. In a 2001 interview, Hebb refuted a story on the Internet stating he had recently graduated from medical school. Rather he completed a night-school course offered by Boston University's School of Medicine. Hebb also cast doubt on a commonly reported belief that the inspiration for "Sunny" was the 1963 death of his brother, Hal. "A lot of people think that," he said. "That could have been—I do not know . . . I cannot confirm that."

**8.6 A. Tommy Boyce & Bobby Hart**

Written by the duo, "I Wonder What She's Doing Tonite" peaked at #8 on February 24, 1968, and was the pair's only record to crack the Top 20. Boyce and Hart were, however, prolific writers whose infectious pop songs were hits for other artists. In 1961 Boyce co-wrote a #7 tune, "Pretty Little Angel Eyes," with its singer, Curtis Lee. Three years later "Come A Little Bit Closer," which Boyce and Hart wrote with Wes Farrell, crept up to #3 for Jay & The Americans. But Boyce and Hart's best-known songs were performed by The Monkees, including the "Theme From The Monkees" and Top 20 hits such as "(I'm Not Your) Steppin' Stone," "Valleri," "Words," and "Last Train To Clarksville," which stopped at the top of the *Billboard* Hot 100 on November 5, 1966.

**8.7 C. Bobby Taylor & The Vancouvers**

Peaking at #29 on the *Billboard* Hot 100 on May 25, 1968, "Does Your Mama Know About Me" was the sole hit for Bobby Taylor & The Vancouvers, an R&B sextet that was signed to Motown subsidiary Gordy Records after Diana Ross heard the group at a nightclub in its hometown, Vancouver, Canada. The song, which addressed interracial romance, was co-written by Tommy Chong, one of the band's guitar players. Chong, who became a counter-culture hero in the 1970s as part of Cheech & Chong, was the second Vancouvers' guitarist to make it big after leaving the group. The first, Jimi Hendrix, was fired shortly after joining the band in December 1962 because, as Bobby Taylor remembers, "his solos went on too long . . . and he played his guitar so loud you couldn't hear the rest of the band." After both follow-up singles to "Does Your Mama Know About Me" failed to crack the Top 40, Bobby Taylor & The Vancouvers disbanded, but not before Taylor discovered five then unknown brothers playing on the same bill as his group at Chicago's Regal Theatre. Taylor introduced the quintet from Gary, Indiana, to Motown's Berry Gordy, Jr., who signed the youngsters and launched their career as the Jackson 5.

**8.8 C. The Jaggerz**

If not for "Bridge Over Troubled Water," The Jaggerz might have topped the *Billboard* Hot 100; instead the band's hit single, "The Rapper," pulled into the #2 spot behind the Simon & Garfunkel classic on March 21, 1970. The sextet from Beaver Falls, Pennsylvania—a suburb of Pittsburgh that is best known as Joe Namath's birthplace—followed up its hit with a pair of releases that rose no higher than #75. "The Rapper," a song about a talkative and persistent pickup artist, was penned by the band's lead singer and guitarist, Dominic Ierace, who resurfaced a decade later as Donnie Iris. In 1981 Iris returned to the chart with a #29 tune, the memorable "Ah! Leah!"

. . . . . . . . . . . . . . . . . . . . . .

**8.9**  D. "Which Way You Goin' Billy?"

Led by Terry Jacks, the Vancouver-based Poppy Family had
released two moderately successful singles in western Canada
before "Which Way You Goin' Billy?," a song originally
intended as a B-side, topped the Canadian chart in 1969.
Inspired by images of young men leaving for Vietnam, Terry
wrote the tune that featured his wife, Susan's, plaintive plea to
a departing boyfriend; it peaked at #2 on the *Billboard* Hot
100 on June 6, 1970. Although the follow-up single, "That's
Where I Went Wrong," reached #29 in the U.S., The Poppy
Family never cracked the Top 40 again. In 1974, however,
after his divorce from Susan, Terry's adaptation of Jacques
Brel's "Seasons In The Sun" became the all-time best-selling
single by a Canadian artist, topping the chart in the U.S.,
Canada, Britain, and several other countries.

**8.10**  B. Climax

A wistful ballad, "Precious And Few" peaked at #3 on
the *Billboard* Hot 100 for Climax on February 26, 1972.
The song, Climax's chart debut, was written by the group's
guitarist, Walter Nims, and sung by Sonny Geraci. In
the mid-1960s Geraci belonged to the Cleveland-based
Outsiders (not to be confused with identically named British
and Dutch bands) and was the voice on that group's four Top
40 tunes, including their biggest hit, "Time Won't Let Me,"
which rose to #5 on April 16, 1966. Nims joined a later
incarnation of The Outsiders before he and Geraci formed
Climax in 1970. Although Climax never again reached the
Top 40, "Rock And Roll Heaven," a tune co-written by the
group's keyboard player John Stevenson and included on
the band's 1972 album, *Climax,* was a #3 hit in 1974 for
The Righteous Brothers.

**8.11** **B. Danny O'Keefe**

"Good Time Charlie's Got The Blues," a brooding ballad about abandonment, reached #9 on the *Billboard* Hot 100 on November 4, 1972. It was the first and last time O'Keefe graced the pop chart, although through the years he has appeared on the Adult Contemporary chart. A number of prominent artists, including Elvis Presley, Willie Nelson, and Mel Torme, have covered "Good Time Charlie," and performers such as Judy Collins, Jimmy Buffett, and Jackson Browne have recorded other O'Keefe compositions. Recently, the Seattle-based singer-songwriter has divided his time between his music and the Songbird Foundation, an organization he founded to promote coffee that is grown without destroying the habitat of endangered songbirds.

**8.12** **D. Stories**

In early 1973 "Brother Louie," the story of a white man with a black girlfriend and racist parents, was a Top 10 hit in Britain for Hot Chocolate, a mixed-race group that included Errol Brown and Tony Wilson, the song's writers. The Stories, meanwhile, were working on their *About Us* album that spring and decided to record the British hit. The Stories' version was on the *Billboard* Hot 100 for 18 weeks, topping the list on August 25. Unable to follow up the success of "Brother Louie," the group disbanded. Lead singer Ian Lloyd recorded a couple of solo albums before embarking on a career as a studio vocalist; he can be heard as a background singer on albums by Foreigner, Peter Frampton, and Billy Joel, among others.

**8.13** **B. "Rock Your Baby"**

George McCrae's timing couldn't have been better: just days after Harry Casey and Richard Finch, the writers and producers of "Rock Your Baby," had finished laying down the song's instrumental tracks, McCrae dropped by T.K. Records' studio in Hialeah, Florida, looking for material to record. On July 13, 1974, with McCrae's vocals, "Rock Your Baby" topped the chart and, along with "Rock The Boat," the Hues Corporation song that it succeeded at #1, became one of the first hits of the disco era. Although McCrae recorded a number of other tunes with Casey and Finch, his subsequent offerings never rose above #37; Casey and Finch fared better, however, scoring five chart-toppers with KC And The Sunshine Band.

**8.14  C. Santa Esmeralda**

On February 18, 1978, Santa Esmeralda's disco arrangement of "Don't Let Me Be Misunderstood," which featured the vocals of Leroy Gomez, peaked at #15 on *Billboard*'s Hot 100, the same rank achieved by The Animals' version 13 years earlier. Buoyed by the success of "Don't Let Me Be Misunderstood," Santa Esmeralda recorded another song popularized by The Animals—"The House Of The Rising Sun"—but it stalled at #78 later the same year.

**8.15  D. Billy Vera & The Beaters**

"At This Moment" almost never had its moment. Originally recorded live at the Roxy in Los Angeles by Vera and his group, which included former Steely Dan and Doobie Brothers guitarist Jeff "Skunk" Baxter, the ballad stumbled to #79 on October 3, 1981. Four years later, in the fall of 1985, "At This Moment" was featured on NBC-TV's *Family Ties* when Michael J. Fox's character, Alex, declared his love for Ellen, played by Tracy Pollan, as she was about to marry another man. Finally on October 2, 1986, when the song was reprised on *Family Ties*, fans of the show began calling radio stations requesting the tune. More than five years after its debut, the single was re-issued, and on January 24, 1987, "At This Moment" topped the *Billboard* Hot 100.

# Game **D**

## Rockin' Little Numbers Crossword

• • • • • • •

In "Wonderful World," Sam Cooke claims not to know a
lot about trigonometry and algebra. Other artists, though,
have shown more of a flair for figures. Solve the puzzle
using rock 'n' roll numbers, including those found in names
of songs, albums, and groups. *(Solutions on page 120.)*

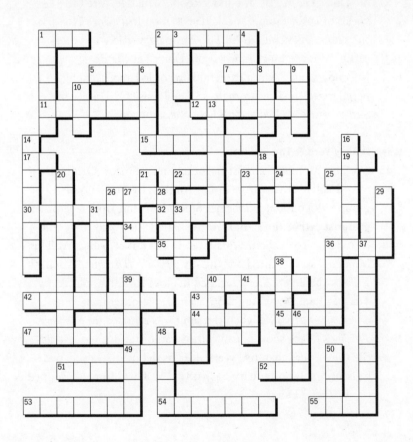

## Across

1. Lovin' Spoonful's "_____ O'Clock"
2. Singer/actress Suzi _____
5. 60s group Count _____
7. Rosanne Cash's "_____ Year Ache"
11. Billy Preston's "Nothing From _____"
12. Jimmy Charles' "_____ To One"
15. "_____ Of Never"
17. Sammy Hagar's "I Can't Drive _____"
19. "_____ Love Affair"
22. "_____ Commandments Of Love"
23. Prince's year
25. Stray Cats' "(She's) Sexy + _____"
26. Van Halen LP
30. Chicago's "Questions _____ _____ _____"
32. Elton John's '80 LP _____ _____ _____
34. Dylan LP Highway _____ Revisited
35. Eric Clapton LP _____ Ocean Boulevard
36. "_____ Nervous Breakdown"
40. Early Elton John LP _____-_____-_____
42. Armed Southern rockers
43. "_____ Ways To Leave Your Lover"
44. "Also Sprach Zarathustra (_____)"
45. Dolly Parton's "_____ _____ _____" movie theme
47. Johnny Rivers' "_____ Son"
49. Amazing Rhythm Aces' "_____ Rate Romance"
51. "Quarter To _____"
52. "_____ Hearts"
53. Dr. Hook's "Only _____"
54. "Future's So Bright" group
55. _____ Tops

## Down

1. "I _____ That Emotion"
3. "Red Red Wine" group
4. Three Dog Night hit
6. "_____ Days A Week"
8. "I'm Henry the _____, I Am"
9. "Love Potion Number _____"
10. Dylan's "Positively _____ Street"
13. Journey LP
14. Chicago hit "_____ _____ _____ _____ _____"
16. Tommy Tutone's "_____-_____/Jenny"
18. Nena's "_____ Luftballons"
20. "Spooky," "Stormy," & "Traces" group
21. Bobby Darin's "_____ Yellow Roses"
23. Fruitgum Co. hit "_____, _____, _____, Red Light"
24. "_____ Tears"
26. Crests' "_____ Candles"
27. Keith's temperature "_____._____"
28. U.K. group Level _____
29. "_____ Street Bridge Song (Feelin' Groovy)"
31. Foreigner hit "_____ Vision"
33. "December, _____ (Oh, What a Night)"
36. Dylan's "Rainy Day Women #_____"
37. "_____ _____ Hours From Tulsa"
38. "Beechwood 4-_____"
39. Alice Cooper song
40. "Joy" by Apollo _____
41. _____ Fruitgum Co.
43. Billy Joel LP _____ Street
46. The Kingston _____
48. "_____ Time Ever I Saw Your Face"
50. Elton John's '83 LP Too Low For _____

. . . . . . . .

**95**

# Girls Just Want To Have Fun

## Women in Rock

• • • • • • • • • • •

I N 1956 Kay Starr's "Rock And Roll Waltz" became the
rock era's first #1 song by a woman. By the early 1960s the
girl groups were regularly topping the chart with now-
classic tunes. And in the 1970s female singer-songwriters,
such as Carole King and Joni Mitchell, were recording best-
selling albums as they took over creative control of their
music. By the mid-1980s Madonna was on her way to
becoming the most successful rock artist of the eighties and
the nineties, as well as one of the most powerful women in
entertainment. Women, no longer rock 'n' roll curiosities,
now stand shoulder-to-shoulder with their male counterparts.

**9.1** **Which song was not a #1 hit for Connie Francis?**
A. "Who's Sorry Now"
B. "Everybody's Somebody's Fool"
C. "My Heart Has A Mind Of Its Own"
D. "Don't Break The Heart That Loves You"

**9.2** Who is known by the nickname "Little Miss Dynamite"?

A. Eva Boyd

B. Brenda Lee

C. Peggy March

D. Millie Small

**9.3** What was the original name of The Supremes?

A. The Carousels

B. The Angels

C. The Primettes

D. The Secrets

**9.4** Who sang lead on The Crystals' 1962 hit, "He's A Rebel"?

A. Cherilyn LaPierre of Caesar and Cleo

B. Barbara Alston of The Crystals

C. La La Brooks of The Crystals

D. Darlene Love of The Blossoms

**9.5** Which singer was also a secretary at Motown Records?

A. Gladys Horton of The Marvelettes

B. Martha Reeves of Martha & The Vandellas

C. Claudette Rogers of The Miracles

D. Mary Wells

**9.6** Which band did Grace Slick sing with?

A. Sweetwater

B. Big Brother & The Holding Company

C. Jefferson Airplane

D. The Full Tilt Boogie Band

**9.7** Which group had a Top 10 hit with "We Are Family" in 1979?

A. Sister Sledge

B. The Pointer Sisters

C. Labelle

D. Rose Royce

**9.8** **Which statement about The Supremes is true?**

A. Their first single as The Supremes reached the Top 10.

B. They had five consecutive #1 singles.

C. After they became Diana Ross and The Supremes in 1967, they never had another #1 hit.

D. "Love Child" was their last chart-topper.

**9.9** **Which song, featuring a female lead vocal, was the last #1 hit of the 1960s?**

A. "Stand By Your Man"

B. "Put A Little Love In Your Heart"

C. "Someday We'll Be Together"

D. "Smile A Little Smile For Me"

**9.10** **Which singer had a Top 10 hit in 1970 with "Lay Down (Candles In The Rain)"?**

A. Joan Baez

B. Melanie

C. Joni Mitchell

D. Linda Ronstadt

**9.11** **Which statement about Carole King is false?**

A. Neil Sedaka wrote "Oh! Carol" for her.

B. She and Paul Simon were students together at New York City's Queens College.

C. *Tapestry* was her first solo album.

D. In general, when writing with Gerry Goffin, she wrote the music, he the lyrics.

**9.12** **Which Top 20 tune launched Kiki Dee's American career in 1974?**

A. "I Am Woman"

B. "Delta Dawn"

C. "I Got The Music In Me"

D. "Never Can Say Goodbye"

**9.13** Who was the female singer on the chart-topping duets, "Up Where We Belong" and "(I've Had) The Time Of My Life"?

A. Jennifer Warnes
B. Buffy Sainte-Marie
C. Tanita Tikaram
D. Nicolette Larson

**9.14** Which group of women, together with vocalist Belinda Carlisle, comprised the Go-Go's?

A. Marge Ganser, Mary Ann Ganser, Betty Weiss, Mary Weiss
B. Rosalind Ashford, Annette Sterling Beard, Gloria Williams
C. Estelle Bennett, Veronica "Ronnie" Bennett, Nedra Talley
D. Charlotte Caffey, Gina Schock, Kathy Valentine, Jane Wiedlin

**9.15** Which all-female group did Joan Jett belong to before she began recording with The Blackhearts?

A. Fanny
B. Vixen
C. The Runaways
D. The New York Dolls

# Answers

• • • • • • • • • • •

**9.1** **A. "Who's Sorry Now"**
Connie Francis had three chart-toppers, but the song she is
best remembered for, "Who's Sorry Now," was not one of
them. Ironically, Francis was very reluctant to record the song,
which peaked at #4 on March 15, 1958. Having already
decided to give up her failing recording career, Francis went to
New York's Olmstead Studios on October 2, 1957, for what
she thought would be the last time. With 20 minutes remain-
ing in the session she decided to record "Who's Sorry Now,"
not because she liked the song—she hated it—but to placate
her father who believed an updated arrangement of the 1923
standard had hit potential because it would be different. The
record didn't generate much interest until New Year's Day
1958, when Dick Clark played it on *American Bandstand* and
paved the way for Francis to become the biggest female
recording star of her era.

**9.2** **B. Brenda Lee**
A little girl with a big voice, Lee performed with an energy
that belied her age and size: she received her nickname at age
12 following the release of her second single, a rollicking rockabilly number called "Dynamite" that peaked at #72 on the
August 10, 1957, pop survey. In 1960, however, she adopted a
more rock-oriented sound that resulted in a dozen Top 10 hits
over the next three years, including the 1960 chart-toppers
"I'm Sorry" and "I Want To Be Wanted." After her pop audience waned in the mid-1960s, Lee returned to her roots and
churned out country hits for the next decade. Although she
stands just 4'9" as an adult, Lee remains one of the biggest
female stars of the rock era.

**9.3** **C. The Primettes**

In 1959 Milton Jenkins, the manager of a male trio called The Primes, moved with his group from Cleveland to Detroit. Once there he met an aspiring singer named Florence Ballard and asked her to assemble a sister group for The Primes. Ballard recruited three other teenaged singers, including future Supremes Mary Wilson and Diane Ross, and Jenkins dubbed them The Primettes. Although the girls auditioned for Berry Gordy, Jr. at Motown Records, he refused to sign them until they had finished high school. Instead, they recorded an uncharted single in 1960 for Lupine Records. Then in January 1961 Gordy signed the group but insisted on a name change; Ballard suggested the new moniker. In 1968 The Supremes, the most successful female group of the rock era, recorded a #2 hit, "I'm Gonna Make You Love Me," with The Temptations, an act that included two original members of The Primes.

**9.4** **D. Darlene Love of The Blossoms**

The Crystals were one of the first girl groups to record with Phil Spector, but the Brooklyn-based quartet had a fallout over money with the legendary producer. Spector had moved west to Los Angeles when he recorded "He's A Rebel," and he recruited Love, a local session singer, and her group, The Blossoms, for the vocals. Spector, however, released the song under The Crystals' name, which he owned, and on November 3, 1962, "He's A Rebel" topped the *Billboard* Hot 100. The group's next Top 10 hit, 1963's "Da Doo Ron Ron (When He Walked Me Home)," featured an actual Crystal, La La Brooks, on lead vocals with Cherilyn LaPierre—a young Cher—singing background.

## 9.5 B. Martha Reeves of Martha & The Vandellas

After winning a talent contest in October 1961, Martha Reeves was asked by a Motown scout, Mickey Stevenson, to audition for the fledgling record label. When she arrived at the studio the next day it was obvious that Stevenson, who didn't have a secretary, needed one. So Reeves began answering the phone and before the day was through, Stevenson had hired her. She supplemented her $35 per week secretarial salary by singing harmonies, for which she was paid $5 per session. When Marvin Gaye's regular background singers were unavailable for the recording of "Stubborn Kind Of Fellow" in July 1962, Reeves recruited her former group, The Del-Phis, for the session. On a later occasion Reeves stood in for Mary Wells during the taping of "I'll Have To Let Him Go" and was impressive enough that Motown owner Berry Gordy, Jr. decided to release her version of the song. Soon after, Gordy signed Reeves and The Del-Phis, and Martha & The Vandellas were born.

## 9.6 C. Jefferson Airplane

Jefferson Airplane emerged as the preeminent psychedelic rock group of the late 1960s when Grace Slick enlisted as one of the group's lead singers in 1966. Before she joined the band, the Airplane had recorded an unheralded folk-rock album. Slick, a former model, gave the band a powerful female voice as well as a visual focus. She also brought with her two songs that she had performed with her first group, The Great Society. "White Rabbit," which she wrote, and "Somebody To Love" would both become Top 10 hits in 1967 for her new outfit. Slick continued with Jefferson Airplane until it broke up in 1973; she also performed with two later incarnations of the band, Jefferson Starship and Starship. In the mid-1980s Slick sang duets with Mickey Thomas on two Starship chart-toppers, "We Built This City" and "Nothing's Gonna Stop Us Now."

**9.7**  A. Sister Sledge

Although the four Sledge sisters—Debbie, Kim, Joni, and
Kathie—had been recording since 1971, their highest position on the *Billboard* Hot 100 prior to 1979 was #92. For the
*We Are Family* album, however, the sisters teamed with Nile
Rodgers and Bernard Edwards, the founders of the trendset-
ting disco act Chic. The result was two Top 10 hits for the
Philadelphia-based Sister Sledge in 1979: in May, "He's The
Greatest Dancer" reached #9 and in June, "We Are Family"
peaked at #2. Both songs, which were written and produced
by Rodgers and Edwards, also topped the R&B chart. Baseball
fans remember "We Are Family" as the theme song of the
1979 World Series champion Pittsburgh Pirates.

**9.8**  B. They had five consecutive #1 singles.

Although The Supremes signed with Tamla, a Motown subsidiary, in early 1961, it would take more than three years for
the group to achieve any significant chart success. Their first
eight singles earned the singers one Top 40 tune, "When The
Lovelight Starts Shining Through His Eyes," #23 on January
11, 1964, and a disparaging nickname, the "No-Hit
Supremes." On April 8, 1964, however, the trio recorded a
song that The Marvelettes had rejected, "Where Did Our Love
Go," which hit #1 on August 22, becoming the first of five
consecutive chart-toppers The Supremes would collect in the
next 10 months. The five songs, all written by Brian Holland,
Lamont Dozier, and Eddie Holland, included "Baby Love,"
"Stop! In The Name Of Love," "Come See About Me," and
"Back In My Arms Again."

**9.9**  C. "Someday We'll Be Together"

When The Supremes ascended to the top position on the
*Billboard* Hot 100 on December 27, 1969, it marked both the
close of a decade and the end of an era. "Someday We'll Be

Together" was the last of the trio's 12 chart-topping hits, and the wistfully titled tune was the final one that Diana Ross would record with the group. The other songs were all Top 20 in 1969: Tammy Wynette stood by her man at the #19 spot, Jackie DeShannon scored a #4 hit with "Put A Little Love In Your Heart," and "Smile A Little Smile For Me" landed at #5 for The Flying Machine, an all-male group.

### 9.10 B. Melanie

Although female acts were a distinct minority at Woodstock, the two best-known songs inspired by the momentous 1969 rock festival were penned by women. After performing her two-song set at Woodstock on the evening of Friday, August 15, Melanie was moved by the thousands of soaked spectators who, responding to a stage announcer's suggestion, held candles skyward in an attempt to stop the rain. She commemorated her experience that night in "Lay Down (Candles In The Rain)," and on July 11, 1970, the tune hit #6 on the *Billboard* Hot 100 for Melanie and The Edwin Hawkins Singers. Two months earlier on May 9, Crosby, Stills & Nash's interpretation of Joni Mitchell's "Woodstock" peaked at #11.

### 9.11 C. *Tapestry* was her first solo album.

Carole King made two long-players before her multimillion-selling breakthrough, *Tapestry*. In 1968, as a member of a trio called The City, she recorded *Now That Everything's Been Said*. Although the album was not a commercial success, it included "That Old Sweet Roll," a tune King wrote with Gerry Goffin that, known by its subtitle, "Hi-De-Ho," became a #14 hit in 1970 for Blood, Sweat & Tears. Her next effort, 1970's *Writer*, was King's first solo album. Despite a guest appearance by James Taylor and the presence of 11 Goffin-King compositions including their classic, "Up On The Roof," the disc failed to find an audience.

**9.12 C. "I Got The Music In Me"**

Although British soul singer Kiki Dee began recording in 1963 at the age of 16, it wasn't until she signed with Elton John's Rocket Records 10 years later that her career took off. "I Got The Music In Me," written by Dee's keyboard player, Bias Boshell, was the first single from her second Rocket album. Following the song's release, Dee opened for John on his U.S. tour, and "I Got The Music In Me" peaked at #12 on November 30, 1974. Dee earned her first #1 record in August 1976 when "Don't Go Breaking My Heart" topped the charts simultaneously in the U.S. and Britain. Somewhat surprisingly, it was the first time her accompanist, Elton John, had captured the top spot in his home country.

**9.13 A. Jennifer Warnes**

In May 1977, a decade after she began her professional singing career, Warnes became an "overnight success" when her first charted single, "Right Time Of The Night," peaked at #6 on the *Billboard* Hot 100. Five years later, despite having lent her voice in 1979 to "It Goes Like It Goes," the uncharted Academy Award–winning song from the movie *Norma Rae*, Warnes' career seemed to have stalled. But then, with Joe Cocker, she recorded "Up Where We Belong," a duet from *An Officer And A Gentleman* that topped the chart for three weeks in November 1982. Warnes hit #1 again in November 1987 with "(I've Had) The Time Of My Life," the love theme from *Dirty Dancing* that she sang with Righteous Brother Bill Medley. Both duets won Academy Awards for Best Original Song, giving the former one-hit wonder an Oscar triple-play.

**9.14 D. Charlotte Caffey, Gina Schock, Kathy Valentine, Jane Wiedlin**

The new-wave pop quintet, known for Top 10 hits such as "We Got The Beat" and "Vacation," was founded as the Misfits in 1978 by Belinda Carlisle, Caffey (lead guitar/keyboards),

Wiedlin (guitar/vocals), and two others. Schock (drums) and Valentine (bass) had joined the Los Angeles–based band by the time it released its first album, *Beauty And The Beat*, in 1981. After the Go-Go's disbanded in 1985, Carlisle enjoyed four Top 10 singles as a solo artist, including the 1987 chart-topper "Heaven Is A Place On Earth."

**9.15   C. The Runaways**

One of the original "grrrl" groups, The Runaways played an abrasive amalgam of pop, punk, and metal that proved women could rock. Formed in 1975, the Los Angeles–based quintet's first three albums were produced by Kim Fowley, who co-produced "Alley-Oop," a #1 hit for the Hollywood Argyles in 1960; nevertheless, The Runaways were largely ignored in the U.S., though they were well received in Japan and Europe. Two members of The Runaways launched successful solo careers after the band broke up in 1979. Lita Ford scored a #8 tune in 1989 with "Close My Eyes Forever," a duet with Ozzy Osbourne. Joan Jett, meanwhile, reeled off a string of Top 40 hits beginning with "I Love Rock 'N Roll," which topped the *Billboard* Hot 100 for seven weeks in 1982.

# *Game* E

## AKA—Also Known As

• • • • • • •

Match the artists' birth name to their stage name.
*(Solutions on page 120.)*

| | | | |
|---|---|---|---|
| **1.** | Steven Georgiou | **A.** | Del Shannon |
| **2.** | Brenda Mae Tarpley | **B.** | Alice Cooper |
| **3.** | Charles Westover | **C.** | Joni Mitchell |
| **4.** | Sharon Myers | **D.** | Chubby Checker |
| **5.** | Vincent Furnier | **E.** | Cat Stevens |
| **6.** | Anna Mae Bullock | **F.** | Joan Jett |
| **7.** | Daryl Dragon | **G.** | Mama Cass Elliot |
| **8.** | Roberta Joan Anderson | **H.** | The Captain |
| **9.** | Gordon Sumner | **I.** | Tina Turner |
| **10.** | Ellen Naomi Cohen | **J.** | Bob Dylan |
| **11.** | Ernest Evans | **K.** | Brenda Lee |
| **12.** | Mary O'Brien | **L.** | Jackie DeShannon |
| **13.** | Robert Zimmerman | **M.** | Sting |
| **14.** | Joan Larkin | **N.** | John Denver |
| **15.** | Henry John Deutschendorf, Jr. | **O.** | Dusty Springfield |

# The Show is Over
## Rock 'n' Roll Heaven
· · · · · · · · · · ·

**R**OCK 'N' ROLL legends are frequently born of tragedy. Although some musicians have been lost to natural causes, many other rockers have died sensational deaths resulting from airplane or automobile crashes, murders, drownings, and other misadventures. Sadly, a large number have been victims of self-destructive behavior, including Russian roulette, suicide, and drug or alcohol abuse. And while the causes of death vary, the passing of rock stars, such as Buddy Holly, Jim Morrison, or John Lennon, often leads to their being idolized more in death than in life. Ultimately, though, their epitaphs are the musical legacies that they leave behind.

**10.1 Where did Buddy Holly die?**
A. Clear Lake, Iowa
B. Lubbock, Texas
C. Fargo, North Dakota
D. Moorhead, Minnesota

· · · · · · · ·

**10.2** Who died less than two years after recording his biggest American hit, "Summertime Blues"?

A. Buddy Knox

B. Eddie Cochran

C. Gene Vincent

D. Johnny Burnette

**10.3** How did Sam Cooke die?

A. Suicide

B. Automobile accident

C. Gun shot

D. Airplane crash

**10.4** What was Otis Redding's intended destination when he was killed in a 1967 plane crash?

A. Dawson, Georgia

B. Madison, Wisconsin

C. Memphis, Tennessee

D. San Francisco, California

**10.5** Whose self-penned epitaph reads, "Please don't judge me too harshly"?

A. Keith Moon

B. Bobby Fuller

C. Brian Jones

D. John Bonham

**10.6** Which statement about Jimi Hendrix is false?

A. "Purple Haze" was his only U.S. Top 10 single.

B. He was the opening act on a 1967 tour with The Monkees.

C. He was born in Seattle.

D. He performed at the Monterey Pop Festival and at Woodstock.

**10.7** Which artist had his/her only *Billboard* #1 hit after his/her death?
  A. Minnie Riperton
  B. Marvin Gaye
  C. Janis Joplin
  D. Andy Gibb

**10.8** Where was The Doors' lead singer, Jim Morrison, when he died?
  A. Los Angeles
  B. Paris
  C. London
  D. Miami

**10.9** According to Don McLean's 1971 epic, "American Pie," on which day did the music die?
  A. October 8, 1958
  B. February 3, 1959
  C. April 17, 1960
  D. November 22, 1963

**10.10** When The Mamas & The Papas re-formed in 1982, who replaced the late Cass Elliot?
  A. Nicolette Larson
  B. Michelle Gilliam
  C. Elaine McFarlane
  D. Mackenzie Phillips

**10.11** Where was Elvis Presley's last live concert?
  A. Lincoln, Nebraska
  B. Madison, Wisconsin
  C. Cincinnati, Ohio
  D. Indianapolis, Indiana

**10.12** How did Jim Croce die?

A. Suicide

B. Automobile accident

C. Drug overdose

D. Airplane crash

**10.13** What was John Lennon's only U.S. #1 hit as a solo artist before his death on December 8, 1980?

A. "Imagine"

B. "Instant Karma (We All Shine On)"

C. "Whatever Gets You Thru The Night"

D. "Stand By Me"

**10.14** What instrument did the late Karen Carpenter, singer for The Carpenters, play?

A. Drums

B. Piano/Keyboards

C. Guitar

D. She was a vocalist only

**10.15** Which departed rock 'n' roll personality was originally known as Bob Smith?

A. Tiny Tim

B. Wolfman Jack

C. Commander Cody

D. ? (of ? And The Mysterians)

# Answers

• • • • • • • • • • •

**10.1**  **A. Clear Lake, Iowa**

Buddy Holly's chartered plane, which he shared with Ritchie
Valens and the Big Bopper, J.P. Richardson, crashed in a
farmer's field 5.4 miles north of Clear Lake, shortly after it
took off in a snowstorm from the Mason City (Iowa) Municipal
Airport at about 1:00 A.M. on Tuesday, February 3, 1959.
The three stars, who along with The Crickets, Dion and The
Belmonts, and Frankie Sardo, had performed in Clear Lake
on Monday evening, were flying to Fargo, North Dakota,
for a Tuesday night show in nearby Moorhead, Minnesota.
The Civil Aeronautics Board found the crash was caused by
pilot error.

**10.2**  **B. Eddie Cochran**

Now a rock 'n' roll classic, "Summertime Blues" was
Cochran's highest-charting single in the U.S., peaking at #8
on the *Billboard* Hot 100 on September 29, 1958. An excellent guitarist with rockabilly roots, Cochran had just finished
touring Britain with Gene Vincent when he was killed near
London on April 17, 1960—Easter Sunday—when the car
taking him to the airport for a flight home to the U.S.
crashed. Following his death "Three Steps To Heaven," which
failed to chart in the U.S., reached #1 in Britain, a country
where Cochran was—and remains—much more popular than
at home. In 1994 "Summertime Blues" topped the country
chart for Alan Jackson.

**10.3**  **C. Gun shot**

The son of a Baptist preacher, Sam Cooke, 33, was a gospel
singer turned pop star who died ignominiously in the early-
morning hours of December 11, 1964, in Los Angeles.

. . . . . . . . . . . . . . . . . . . . . . . . . .

Cooke, whose Top 10 hits included "Chain Gang," Twistin' The Night Away," and the chart-topping "You Send Me," was shot in the heart by Bertha Franklin, the 55-year-old manager of the rundown Hacienda Motel in Watts, following a struggle in the motel office. The singer, who was intoxicated, had apparently broken into the office in a fruitless search for the woman with whom he had checked in less than 45 minutes earlier. Cooke's companion, allegedly a prostitute, told police that the singer had kidnapped her. A coroner's inquest ruled the death a justifiable homicide. His second funeral—the first was in Chicago—at Los Angeles' Mount Sinai Baptist Church featured performances by Bobby "Blue" Bland, Billy Preston, Lou Rawls, and Ray Charles.

**10.4** **B. Madison, Wisconsin**
Otis Redding's twin-engine Beechcraft was flying from Cleveland to Madison on December 10, 1967, when it plunged, approximately four miles short of its destination, into Lake Monona, claiming seven, including the singer and four members of his touring band, the Bar-Kays (one member of the band survived the crash). Only 26 years old when he was killed, Redding was on the cusp of stardom. Six months earlier, on June 3, Aretha Franklin's cover of his song "Respect" topped the *Billboard* Hot 100. Two weeks after that, Redding played the Monterey Pop Festival to rave reviews. Then on November 22—not December 7 as is commonly reported—18 days before he died, Redding recorded "(Sittin' On) The Dock Of The Bay," which topped the chart for four weeks starting March 16, 1968. The song, which he was inspired to write in August 1967 while staying on a houseboat at Waldo Point Harbor in Sausalito, traces Redding's life from his humble roots in Georgia to the San Francisco Bay area, where at Monterey he achieved his greatest professional success.

### 10.5 C. Brian Jones

Less than a month after Jones announced his departure from The Rolling Stones, the group's original lead guitarist was found dead in his swimming pool. A coroner ruled that Jones "drowned under the influence of alcohol and drugs." On July 5, 1969, two days after the guitarist's death, The Stones, with Mick Taylor in Jones' stead, played a scheduled free concert for more than 250,000 people in London's Hyde Park. Before the performance the band paid tribute to Jones, releasing 3,500 butterflies near the stage after Mick Jagger read two stanzas from *Adonais*, Shelley's elegy to Keats. Jones was buried on July 10 in a cemetery near his family's home in Cheltenham.

### 10.6 A. "Purple Haze" was his only U.S. Top 10 single.

Although Jimi Hendrix is now an American rock 'n' roll legend, during his lifetime his music did not chart well in the U.S.: his highest-ranked single was a cover of Bob Dylan's "All Along The Watchtower," which reached #20 on the *Billboard* Hot 100 on October 19, 1968. In Britain, however, Hendrix was much more successful, racking up four Top 10 hits between 1966 and 1970, including "Purple Haze," a #65 tune in the U.S. that peaked at #3 on the other side of the Atlantic in May 1967. Ironically it was in London, the city where his enormous talents were first recognized, that Hendrix died from "barbiturate intoxication" on September 18, 1970.

### 10.7 C. Janis Joplin

All four artists had #1 hits, and all but Joplin were alive when they topped the *Billboard* Hot 100. On March 20, 1971, not quite six months after her death from a heroin overdose, Joplin's rendition of "Me And Bobby McGee" reached #1, where it stayed for two weeks. The song was written by Kris Kristofferson, one of Joplin's former boyfriends, and was recorded by Joplin and The Full Tilt Boogie Band for her album *Pearl*, which was released after she died on October 4, 1970.

**10.8  B. Paris**

Early in the morning of July 3, 1971, Jim Morrison's body
was discovered by his girlfriend, Pamela Courson, in the bath-
tub of their borrowed apartment at Rue Beautreillis 17.
Morrison had been enchanted with Paris when he visited in
1970 and, in March 1971, after he had completed recording
the *L.A. Woman* album, he returned to the French capital to
write. The cause of death was listed as heart failure; however,
no autopsy was performed, leading to speculation that drugs
were involved. Morrison was buried in Paris's Père-Lachaise
Cemetery, the final resting place of many other notable
musical and literary figures, including Molière, Chopin,
Oscar Wilde, and Edith Piaf.

**10.9  B. February 3, 1959**

As a young teenager, Don McLean idolized Buddy Holly.
To McLean, the death of the bespectacled rock 'n' roll pioneer
on February 3, 1959, marked the day the music died. More
than a decade later, though, when McLean chronicled the
decline of rock 'n' roll in "American Pie," Holly's demise
symbolized the music's, and by extension, America's, loss of
innocence: as the mantle of rock's supremacy passed from
Elvis Presley (the king)—who had re-inherited the crown
when Holly died—to Bob Dylan (the jester) to The Beatles
(the sergeants), the idealism of the 1950s' sock hop descended
into the mayhem of the late 1960s' rock festival, specifically,
the murder of a fan at a Rolling Stones concert in 1969.

**10.10  C. Elaine McFarlane**

The original female voices of The Mamas & The Papas were
Cass Elliot and Michelle Gilliam Phillips. After the group
disbanded in the late 1960s, Elliot, 33, died on July 29, 1974,
of a heart attack while in London, England. In 1982 the
group re-formed as The New Mamas & Papas, and founder
John Phillips recruited two new women singers. He replaced

his former wife, Michelle Gilliam Phillips, with his daughter from an earlier marriage, Mackenzie Phillips, who as an actress had a principal role on the late-1970s TV sitcom *One Day At A Time*. Elliot's place in the group was taken by Elaine "Spanky" McFarlane, the former lead singer of the folk-pop ensemble Spanky And Our Gang, which was best known for "Sunday Will Never Be The Same," a #9 song in 1967.

**10.11  D. Indianapolis, Indiana**

Elvis Presley's last concert took place in front of more than 18,000 fans on June 26, 1977, at the Market Square Arena in Indianapolis. Although The King was overweight and at times seemed confused when addressing the audience, he reportedly had fun as he performed a 20-song set that included classics such as "Jailhouse Rock," "(Let Me Be Your) Teddy Bear," "Don't Be Cruel," and "Hound Dog," as well as a couple of tunes—"Release Me" and "Bridge Over Troubled Water"— that he seldom sang. The last song Elvis performed was "Can't Help Falling In Love." On August 17, the day after he died, Elvis was scheduled to play in Portland, Maine, the first of a short series of shows that would have concluded with a concert in Memphis 11 days later.

**10.12  D. Airplane crash**

After performing at Northwestern State University in Natchitoches, Louisiana, on September 20, 1973, Jim Croce, along with his lead guitarist, Maury Muehleisen, and four others, was killed when his small chartered plane hit a tree while taking off. Success had arrived late for the 30-year-old singer: he spent a decade working blue-collar jobs, collecting real-life experiences that he would weave into engaging story-songs like "Bad, Bad Leroy Brown," which topped the *Billboard* Hot 100 on July 21, 1973. Eight days before his death, ABC broadcast *She Lives*, a made-for-TV movie featuring "Time In A

Bottle," Croce's reflective ballad about the inevitability of time. Viewer response to the song, combined with an emotional outpouring following Croce's passing, propelled "Time In A Bottle" to the top of the chart on December 29, 1973.

**10.13 C. "Whatever Gets You Thru The Night"**

After the breakup of The Beatles, Lennon had two chart-toppers in the U.S.: "(Just Like) Starting Over," his second, was at #6 on the *Billboard* Hot 100 when he was murdered; it climbed to the top of the survey on December 27, 1980. "Whatever Gets You Thru The Night" was recorded in August 1974 and featured Elton John on piano, organ, and backing vocals. The musician's cameo was in return for Lennon's appearance a month earlier—as Dr. Winston O'Boogie—playing guitar on John's recording of Lennon's composition "Lucy In The Sky With Diamonds." On November 28, 12 days after "Whatever Gets You Thru The Night" went to #1, Elton John performed at New York's Madison Square Garden and was joined on stage by Lennon for three numbers: "Whatever Gets You Thru The Night," "Lucy In The Sky With Diamonds," and The Beatles' early classic, "I Saw Her Standing There." It was Lennon's last concert appearance.

**10.14 A. Drums**

Karen Carpenter, the voice behind chart-toppers such as "(They Long To Be) Close To You," "Top Of The World," and "Please Mr. Postman," plus more than a dozen other Top 20 hits, learned to play drums while attending Downey (California) High School. Before she and her piano-playing older brother Richard formed their Grammy Award–winning duo in 1968, they performed together in a jazz trio and a rock band, with Karen doubling as a drummer and vocalist. Karen continued to beat the skins with The Carpenters—she's credited as a drummer on most Carpenters' albums—but as the act became increasingly popular she stepped out from behind the drum kit and took center stage as lead singer. After battling anorexia nervosa for more than seven years, Karen Carpenter, 32, succumbed to a heart attack on February 4, 1983.

**10.15  B. Wolfman Jack**
Between—and often during—the R&B records he played in the mid- to late-1960s, Robert Weston Smith howled at the moon and exhorted his audience to "git nekkid." Broadcast from high-powered pirate radio stations based in Mexico, Wolfman Jack's late-night radio show could be heard, on a clear night, throughout western North America. Ironically it was visual media, not radio, that cemented his legendary reputation in the 1970s: in 1973 he played a disc jockey in George Lucas's blockbuster movie, *American Graffiti*, and began an eight-year run as host of NBC-TV's *The Midnight Special*. "Clap For The Wolfman," a #6 hit in 1974 for The Guess Who, featured a cameo by the legendary deejay. Wolfman Jack suffered a fatal heart attack on July 1, 1995.


• • • • • • • •

➤ **Your Opinion Matters**

I hope you have enjoyed *Rock 'n' Roll Trivia*. If you have a comment about this book or a suggestion for future editions, please write to me at: rocktrivia@yahoo.com, or *Rock 'n' Roll Trivia*, c/o Greystone Books, 2323 Quebec Street, Suite 201, Vancouver, B.C. Canada V5T 4S7. Although it may not be possible to answer each letter, I promise to read every one.

Thank you,
MICHAEL HARLING

# Game Solutions

• • • • • • • • • • •

*Game A: Going To The Chapel*

1: G / 2: J / 3: L / 4: A / 5: D / 6: M / 7: C / 8: E / 9: K /
10: B / 11: H / 12: I / 13: O / 14: N / 15: F

*Game B: Rock Around the World Crossword*

```
  D E T R O I T           O   H
  U               F   S C O T L A N D
B E L G I U M     R   P     T   R
O   U       I   U A L A S K A   L   B
S   T   L   A   S N   I     W   E   E
T   H   U   M   S C A N A D A   M   L
O       B   I S R A E L   M         F
N       B       A     B   E   C H I C A G O
        O       C A T A L I N A W   S   R
H   N   C A T A L I N A     M   C H I G A N     N
O Z A R K           L O U I S I A N A       O
L   S       L O U I S I A N A   F   H       R
L   H               D       O   H           W
A   V   G   N I G E R I A   R   I           A
N   I   R   P       A       N   N       U   Y
D   L   M A N H A T T A N   I   G       S
    L   C   N   I   A S I A T U L S A
  D E N V E R   E   J       O
        L   M   U T A H   L O N D O N
  A T L A N T A A       H
        N       N   P A L I S A D E S
  B R O A D W A Y       O
```

*Game C: Duets*

1: Jc / 2: Ae or Ea / 3: Di / 4: Gb / 5: Ch / 6: Fg /
7: Ae or Ea / 8: Id / 9: Bj / 10: Kl / 11: Hf / 12: Lk

## Game D: Rockin' Little Numbers Crossword

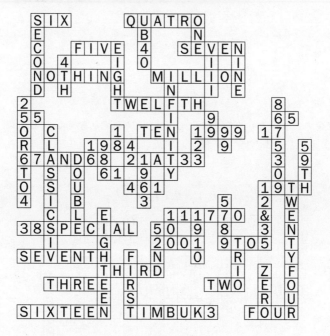

## Game E: AKA—Also Known As

1: E / 2: K / 3: A / 4: L / 5: B / 6: I / 7: H / 8: C / 9: M /
10: G / 11: D / 12: O / 13: J / 14: F / 15: N

# Selected Bibliography

Bowman, Rob. *Soulsville, U.S.A.: The Story of Stax Records.*
New York: Schirmer Books, 1997.

Bronson, Fred. *The Billboard Book of Number One Hits.* 4th ed.
New York: Billboard Books, 1997.

DeCurtis, Anthony and James Henke, editors. *The Rolling
Stone Illustrated History of Rock & Roll.* 3rd ed. New York:
Random House, 1992.

Escott, Colin with Martin Hawkins. *Good Rockin' Tonight:
Sun Records and the Birth of Rock 'n' Roll.* New York:
St. Martin's Press, 1991.

Gordy, Berry. *To Be Loved: The Music, The Magic, The Memories
Of Motown.* New York: Warner Books, 1994.

Jancik, Wayne. *The Billboard Book of One-Hit Wonders.* Revised
ed. New York: Billboard Books, 1998.

Joynson, Vernon. *The Tapestry of Delights.* 3rd ed. Great
Britain: Borderline Books, 1998.

Karpp, Phyllis. *Ike's Boys: The Story of the Everly Brothers.*
Ann Arbor: Pierian Press, 1988.

Kooper, Al with Ben Edmonds. *Backstage Passes: Rock 'n' Roll Life in the Sixties.* New York: Stein and Day, 1977.

Marsh, Dave. *Louie Louie.* New York: Hyperion, 1993.

Otfinoski, Steve. *The Golden Age of Rock Instrumentals.* New York: Billboard Books, 1997.

Rees, Dafydd and Luke Crampton. DK *Encyclopedia of Rock Stars.* New York: DK Publishing, 1996.

Rice, Jo et al. *Guinness Book of 500 Number One Hits.* Middlesex: Guinness Superlatives Ltd., 1982.

Rice, Tim et al. *Guinness Book of Hits of the 60s.* Middlesex: Guinness Superlatives Ltd., 1984.

Russell, Tom and Sylvia Tyson. *And Then I Wrote: The Songwriter Speaks.* Vancouver: Arsenal Pulp Press, 1995.

Shannon, Bob and John Javna. *Behind The Hits.* New York: Warner Books, 1986.

Smith, Joe. *Off The Record: An Oral History of Popular Music.* New York: Warner Books, 1988.

Stambler, Irwin. *The Encyclopedia of Pop, Rock & Soul.* Revised ed. New York: St. Martin's Press, 1989.

Warner, Jay. *The Billboard Book of American Singing Groups: A History 1940–1990.* New York: Billboard Books, 1992.

Whitburn, Joel. *Top Pop Singles 1955–1999.* 9th ed. Menomonee Falls, Wisconsin: Record Research, 2000.

Zollo, Paul. *Songwriters On Songwriting.* Cincinnati: Writer's Digest Books, 1991.